MAPPING THE SILK ROAD

MAPPING THE SILK ROAD

The Riddle of Ptolemy's Stone Tower

RIAZ DEAN

CASEMATE
Pennsylvania & Yorkshire

Published in the United States of America and Great Britain in 2025 by
CASEMATE PUBLISHERS
1950 Lawrence Road, Havertown, PA 19083, USA
and
47 Church Street, Barnsley, S70 2AS, UK

This book was published in India in 2022 titled *The Stone Tower: Ptolemy, the Silk Road, and a 2,000-Year-Old Riddle*.

Copyright 2025 © Riaz Dean
Riaz Dean has asserted his right to be identified as author of the work.

Hardcover Edition: ISBN 978-1-63624-609-3
Digital Edition: ISBN 978-1-63624-610-9

A CIP record for this book is available from the British Library

All rights reserved. No part of this book may be reproduced or transmitted in any form or by any means, electronic or mechanical including photocopying, recording or by any information storage and retrieval system, without permission from the publisher in writing.

Printed and bound in the United Kingdom by CPI Group (UK) Ltd, Croydon, CR0 4YY

Typeset in India by Manipal Technologies Limited, Manipal

For a complete list of Casemate titles, please contact:

CASEMATE PUBLISHERS (US)
Telephone (610) 853-9131
Fax (610) 853-9146
Email: casemate@casematepublishers.com
www.casematepublishers.com

CASEMATE PUBLISHERS (UK)
Telephone (0)1226 734350
Email: casemate@casemateuk.com
www.casemateuk.com

Cover image: Map from Leinhart Holle's 15th-century edition of Ptolemy's *Geographia*.

The Publisher's authorised representative in the EU for product safety is Authorised Rep Compliance Ltd., Ground Floor, 71 Lower Baggot Street, Dublin D02 P593, Ireland.
http://www.arccompliance.com

Again, for Beth

*But the route from the Stone Tower to the Seres (China)
is subject to bad storms . . .*

*. . . not only is there a (return) route from the Seres to Bactria
via the Stone Tower, but also to India . . .*

—Claudius Ptolemy, *Geographia*

Contents

List of Maps	ix
List of Illustrations	x
Introduction	xi

Part One: Birth of the Silk Road

1.	The Grand Historian	3
2.	Barbarians from the North	10
3.	The Journey West	21
4.	Heavenly Horses	32
5.	The First Caravans	44
6.	The Silk Road	56

Part Two: In the Heart of Asia

7.	Migration of the Yuezhi	73
8.	The Kushan Empire	82
9.	Sogdian Traders	95
10.	The Archaeological Explorer	103
11.	The Hidden Library	115

Part Three: Ptolemy's Stone Tower

12. Ptolemy's *Geographia*	135
13. The Data	148
14. The Description	160
15. A New Approach	173
16. Solomon's Throne	186
Epilogue	195
Acknowledgements	197
Appendix	199
Image Credits	201
Timeline of Key Events	202
Glossary	204
Select Bibliography	207
Index	213

Maps

1. The Silk Road: showing central overland routes c. AD 100   2
2. Central Asia: marking the journey of Zhang Qian   23
3. Central Asia: marking the migration path of the Yuezhi   72
4. Vicinity of the Stone Tower: showing likely sites   134
5. Maes's Caravan: showing main route options   163
6. Maes's Caravan: showing distances and elevation   181

All maps above created by Roger Smith of Geographx.

Illustrations

1. The Journey West: Emperor Wu dispatching Zhang Qian 22
2. Remains of the Jade Gate, as seen by author in 2005 39
3. Heavenly Horse: bronze statuette from Later Han period 43
4. Kushan coinage: Kanishka, Buddha, skull deformation 89
5. Aurel Stein and his caravan in the Taklamakan Desert 107
6. Wooden panel depicting the secret of sericulture 112
7. Watchtower where Sogdian Ancient Letters found 118
8. Entrance to Hidden Library with manuscript bundles 123
9. Manuscripts found in the Hidden Library 124
10. Eratosthenes estimating Earth's circumference 140
11. The Stone Tower as man-made structure and mountain 171
12. Two ariel views of Sulaiman-Too 177
13. NASA satellite image showing snowfall levels in Pamirs 179
14. Petroglyph of Heavenly Horse in Ferghana Valley 191
15. UN postage stamp of Sulaiman-Too 191
16. Kushan kings seen emerging from rock on their coins 191
17. Pilgrim trail on Sulaiman-Too 191
18. Ground gutters and cup hollows along trail 191

Introduction

One might ask how this book is different from the many others about the Silk Road. At its heart, it attempts to solve a 2,000-year-old riddle of ancient geography: Where was the now-lost Stone Tower that Ptolemy spoke of, which marked the midpoint on the old Silk Road as caravans plied their trade between Europe and Asia? Once it began functioning sometime around 100 BC, this 'road' would connect two of the great empires of the day—Rome and China—along east–west routes, even as some branched south into India and others would soon include many far-flung kingdoms. Its midpoint was *the* most important landmark for travellers, thus making any search for it intrinsically worthwhile and requiring no further justification. It was here, too, that one of the greatest long-distance caravans in history halted to rest and trade, and its forgotten story is told once more in the pages that follow.

Claudius Ptolemy (circa AD 90–168) is considered the finest scholar of his time; and his work continues to be much studied today, especially by way of the many splendid maps prepared from his rare texts that are housed in museums all around the world. It is from his treatise *Geographia*—an atlas of the ancient world—that our puzzle arises. In it, Ptolemy listed thousands of places extending all the way to the Far East, including a reference to the Stone Tower. This was a special place high up in the mountains, situated somewhere by the doorway into and out of China's western extremity, in a region referred to as the Roof of the World.

A monk during the Middle Ages hunted down a copy of Ptolemy's manuscript, which had by then become lost to the world. Ever since his discovery, the tower's precise location has been vigorously debated by *many* scholars and in multiple languages—so much so, that it is near impossible to review all the material written about it. Until now, however, no *book* has been published with the sole focus of locating this elusive landmark, which, over the centuries, has taken on almost mythical proportions. If its location could be positively identified, then not only would this be of great significance to the study of ancient geography, but it would also allow future archaeological work in this region to be more targeted, thereby increasing the chances of successful excavations. This, in turn, could lead to other settlements and landmarks detailed by Ptolemy also being rediscovered, helping scholars further unlock the history and cartography of many nations.

In 2015, attempting to answer this question, I wrote an article titled 'The Location of Ptolemy's Stone Tower', which appeared in *The Silk Road*, a journal then published by the Silk Road Foundation. Although it provides the basis for this book, my article had to comply with the journal's word limit and academic style. Now, with further research, including new material recently published by others, this topic can be discussed in a more thorough and accessible way with the *general reader* in mind.

As will become evident, only by understanding the wider historical context during this period can this site be located with any certainty. For this reason, this book is divided into three parts: the first explains the birth of the Silk Road; the second covers key events in history that determined the Stone Tower's establishment at the halfway mark; and the third pinpoints where the tower actually was located. Since it stood on a caravan route deep within the heart of Asia, this narrative will not examine coexisting maritime routes although, broadly speaking, they too were a part of this transcontinental Eurasian trade network.

A hundred years before Ptolemy, two neighbouring peoples would begin to gain ascendancy in the region, the Kushans and the Sogdians. The former became one of the first middlemen of a road that would join two continents until then unaware of each other. Kushan merchants would eventually be replaced by their northern neighbour, the Sogdians—an Aryan people, originally from Persia but now living at its northeastern edge (mainly straddling present-day Uzbekistan, Tajikistan and Kyrgyzstan). They, too, became expert merchants and their trading culture is described in this book in a somewhat novel way, by portraying the lives of four generations of caravanners. Yet, even their brief *story*—limited to a paragraph per chapter and shown in *italics*—will endeavour to be historically accurate and provide glimpses of the life of caravanners on the Silk Road.

The timeline we cover spans almost 300 years: It starts in 140 BC, when a Chinese palace guard named Zhang Qian volunteered to travel west for his emperor, in the process founding this celebrated trade route; and it ends in AD 140, when Ptolemy probably completed his *Geographia* and revealed the site of the Stone Tower. For the most part, this period parallels the First Silk Roads Era dating from 100 BC to AD 250 as defined by historian Craig Benjamin, which 'resulted in the most significant transregional commercial and cultural interactions experienced by humans to this point in history'. He goes on to describe it as 'the quintessential example of ancient globalization'. Today, we find modern history often reflecting a Western world bias when apportioning credit for recent human advancements; and sometimes, through omission, even erasing Eastern influences. The history of the Silk Road reminds us why it is wrong to understate the impact of older civilizations, from where it all began centuries earlier.

Any book involving history across nations, by necessity must deal with the names of people and places originating from various languages and scripts. Here, these are spelt or romanized in a way familiar to most (a second, common form is sometimes shown in brackets). In a few cases, ancient names in translations and quotations have also been standardized—without any loss of meaning—so as not to be unduly confusing. And to avoid overwhelming readers with too many names and dates, as far as possible this narrative will only mention the key ones. More so, because this book does not set out to make a detailed study of the various topics covered—rather, with the Silk Road as a backdrop, it attempts to solve the age-old riddle surrounding Ptolemy's lost Stone Tower.

PART ONE
BIRTH OF THE SILK ROAD

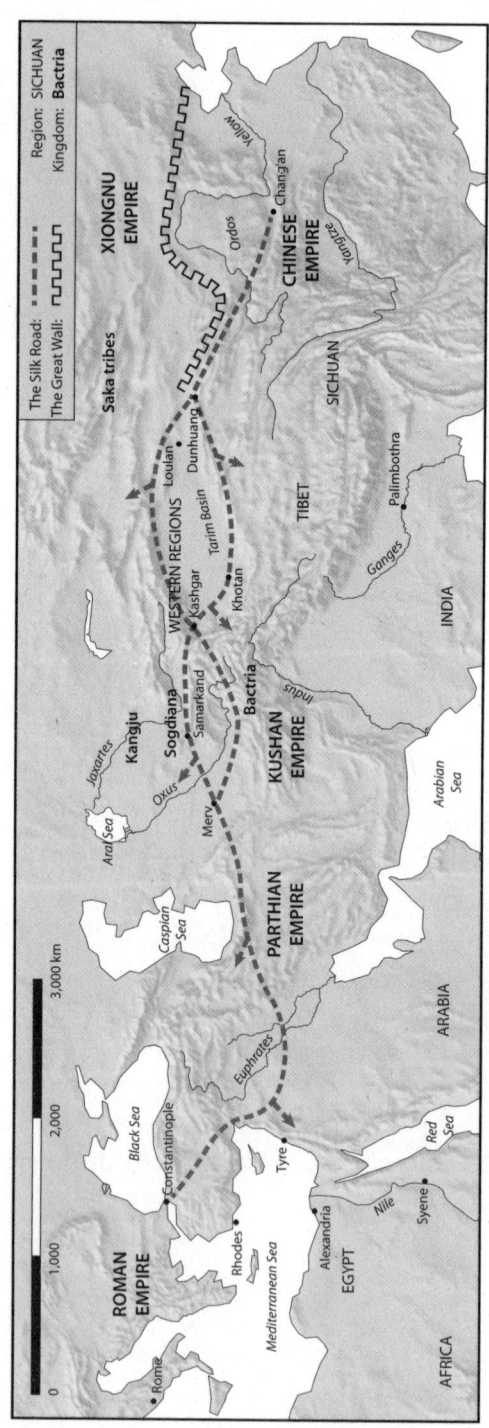

Map 1. The Silk Road: showing central overland routes circa AD 100

1

The Grand Historian

A Chinese empress, so a legend recounts, stumbled onto the secret of making silk. While walking through her garden, she plucked a cocoon off a mulberry tree which she then accidentally dropped into a steaming bowl of tea. As she tried to retrieve it, the cocoon began unravelling to reveal an endless milk-coloured thread—one that would soon be woven into the most sought-after fabric in the world. Her name was Xiling Shi, wife of the semi-mythical ruler Huang Di (meaning 'Yellow Emperor'). He founded the Chinese nation 5,000 years ago and is ancestor to all ethnic Han Chinese. During his rule, which supposedly lasted more than a century, he initiated the calendar, agriculture, music, the arts and sciences to meet his country's needs. Huang Di's mausoleum, which stands north of the modern-day city of Xi'an in Shaanxi province, is still visited by hordes of people each year; while Xiling Shi is referred to as Silkworm Mother and remains a popular object of worship.

Putting aside the legend, sericulture and weaving are thought to have originated over 3,000 years ago in 'the Middle Kingdom'— or *Seres* as the ancient Greeks referred to China, identifying the country with its famed export. Silk production was China's most closely guarded state secret, spawning an industry that would bring it enormous wealth through the ages and continues to do so today. Silk—as skeins of thread or bales of fabric—was the first significant product exported from Asia to Europe. It would ultimately, and for good reason, give this trade route its name when in 1877, a German geographer named Ferdinand von Richthofen coined the phrase *die Seidenstrasse* (the Silk Road). But it ought to be remembered that before this time, no one spoke or thought of 'the road' in this way. Popular and convenient though his description remains, as we now know, it was not *just* a conduit for silk, and nor was there only *one* continuous road. Today, some academics question if this concept of a road is too much of a distraction, and whether such a name should be used at all—historian Alfred Andrea recently answered: 'Yes! There is no good reason to abandon these evocative, albeit inexact, terms. History without romance is sterile.'

The nomad leaned forward on his shaggy pony, watching with curiosity, as he approached the settled people tilling their land on the fringe of the steppe. He and the men of his tribe, though armed with bows and hunting knives, had come to trade. Today, meat and rough wool from their herds to be bartered for metal products, colourful cloth and perhaps a few sweets—essentials and delicacies that their wandering way of life made difficult to produce. How sedentary they looked, tied to their village and its surroundings, when the world beckoned to the north. Were they not prisoners to their walled settlement? Did they not feel the need to ride over the endless grasslands, forever moving with the herds and seeking out lush pastures? But their rough, earthen homes looked warm and inviting, a refuge no doubt from the harsh winter which the nomad's own family knew all too well. Was it only from the exceptional cold last season that he had lost his first-born—a son, no less? Or was it, as the shaman had mumbled as she came out of her trance, to the hungry spirits of the steppe who often took what was not rightly theirs? Either way, memories of the boy's laughter pained him still; there would be no need for sweets in his yurt this summer.

To uncover the main written sources describing the birth of the Silk Road, we must turn to the Chinese annals. The early history of China and the lands to its north and west also record the eternal struggle between the nomadic and settled people. A struggle in which the latter would inevitably prevail, everywhere, for the simple reason offered by science editor Geoffrey Carr: 'But farmers have numbers on their side. And numbers beget numbers, which in turn beget cities.' The Han Dynasty and its cities would be at the forefront of this evolution as it emerged 200 years before the birth of Christ. Although it eventually disintegrated after four centuries of rule, this dynasty would forever shape China and its people. Not only did it give the country's main ethnic group its lasting name, but it also established the basic patterns of China's government and culture, many of which persevere to this day.

Much of the information about the Han comes from the *Shiji* (or *Shih chi*), otherwise known as *Records of the Grand Historian*. It relates the history of this land as chronicled by Sima Qian (or Ssuma Ch'ien)—the Herodotus of China, as he is often referred to. Yet the little we know of his life comes from what he chose to tell us himself. Born around 145 BC, he completed this text, building on material sketched out by his father Sima Tan, thereby fulfilling his dying wish. At his deathbed, then thirty-five years old, Sima Qian records having uttered: 'I, your son, am ignorant and unworthy, but I shall endeavour to set forth in full the reports of antiquity which have come down from our ancestors. I shall not dare to be remiss!'

A gifted scholar and poet, like his father, he was the appointed court historian and astrologer. As the latter, his main duty involved formulating the calendar for the coming year, before presenting it to the emperor prior to the Chinese New Year. It would guide the country's all-important agricultural activities, requiring the correct identification of all auspicious days as well as those fraught with difficulty. Its accuracy not only signalled that the empire was well-governed, but also added to the divinity of the 'Son of Heaven' in the eyes of his people. Conversely, a failure to correctly predict cosmic events was interpreted as a sign of his moral imperfection, which could have serious implications. An apocryphal chapter from Chinese history of this era recounts how two astronomers were sentenced to death for failing to predict the occurrence of an eclipse for their emperor. Acting on Sima Qian's advice that the calendar inherited from the previous Qin Dynasty contained errors, Emperor Wu Di (or Wudi)* ordered its revision in 105 BC. The result was the *Taichu* (Grand Inception) calendar, which was promulgated the following year and now began in January rather than October. It assigned 29.5 days to every month, 365.3 days to the year, and represented the most advanced calendar in the world at the time.

Despite his loyal service to Emperor Wu, there came a time when the Grand Historian fell from grace. It came about after one of the emperor's commanders, General Li Ling, was defeated and captured by the Xiongnu (or Hsiung-nu)—the most powerful tribal confederation amongst the 'northern barbarians' menacing China's borders. Although he was not close to the general, Sima Qian admired the man greatly and spoke out in his defence at the Han court. But, unaware that Li Ling had already defected to the Xiongnu by this stage, the historian unwittingly earned his emperor's wrath, who was sick with rage on hearing of his general's capitulation. Too poor to buy the commutation of his sentence (a common practice then) and lacking friends brave enough to speak up for him, Sima Qian was given a stark choice: to honourably take his own life, as expected of a gentleman, or be castrated. He chose the latter, in order to buy time to fulfil the promise made to his father and complete his life's work. In its final chapter, in one fleeting sentence, he simply mentions: 'I met with the Li Ling catastrophe and was hidden away in a dark cell, bound with ropes.' Later, in a long letter to his friend Jen An (or Ren An), who was awaiting execution, Sima Qian explained his anguish more fully—part of which is reflected here:

> A man has only one death . . . It all depends upon the way he uses it . . . Yet the brave man does not necessarily die for

---

* Wu means 'martial' or 'warlike', while the early Chinese emperors were titled Di.

honour, while even the coward may fulfil his duty . . . If even the lowest slave and scullion maid can bear to commit suicide, why should not one like myself be able to do what has to be done? But the reason I have not refused to bear these ills and have continued to live, dwelling in vileness and disgrace without taking my leave, is that I grieve that I have things in my heart which I have not been able to express fully, and I am shamed to think that after I am gone my writings will not be known to posterity.

According to Burton Watson, who translated the Grand Historian's work: 'Two thousand years of admiring readers have amply rewarded his bitter decision . . . it [the *Shiji*] has been one of the most widely and affectionately read of all Chinese historical works.' While historian John Man describes his letter to Jen An as 'one of the strongest, most heartfelt and moving pieces of writing in Chinese literature'.

Probably written with a brush of rabbit hair dipped in black ink made from pine soot, the 'pages' of the *Shiji* comprised thin bamboo strips bound with string. The completed 'book' contained over half a million characters arranged into 130 chapters. Toiling since his father's death, Sima Qian finished his epic around 94 BC, dying a few years later. More than sixty editions have been printed over the years; but since the oldest extant copy dates back to only the twelfth century, it leaves at least a 1,000-year gap from the original manuscript and raises the real possibility of textual corruption creeping in during the intervening period. Moreover, as Sima Qian himself recorded, his work was hindered by a terrible destruction a century earlier: The first ruler of a unified China had ordered the burning of books, as well as burying alive hundreds of scholars, at odds with his philosophy. Only works consistent with Emperor Qin's interpretation of history were kept in circulation, although a few copies of contradictory texts were locked away in the imperial archives. The Grand Historian should have had access to these, but perhaps not to the originals as many were destroyed in a palace fire after the Han ousted the Qin and only reconstructed later from memory.

Although, more often than not, the *Shiji* is the best historical source available, the facts and quotes recorded by the Grand Historian are sometimes disputed today; Watson notes how 'he relies upon elaborate and probably fictious speeches put into the mouths of his characters to explain and advance the action . . .' According to John Man: 'Real events and outcomes provide a sound historical framework, but it is Sima Qian's invented dialogue and characterization that fill it with life.' Man adds that the records were sometimes 'an oblique way to criticize his own emperor' who had dealt with him so harshly. For example, he praises the previous emperor for setting 'an example for the empire in the simplicity of his way of life' as a way of pointing out current imperial excesses and the ruinous expenditure on war with the barbarians. Since no other contemporary histories have survived Wu's reign, we have only Sima Qian's account to judge his emperor, the man who had him castrated—a situation that leads Watson to point out: 'It is difficult to imagine a more striking and ironical example of the awesome power wielded by historians.'

As scribe for the emperor, Sima Qian toured the country with him and spoke to prominent military officials. From this comes the first accurate description of the Xiongnu, who played a critical role in the country's early history. And he also provides the first eyewitness account of one of the enduring wonders of China; a structure built to keep the barbarians at bay, that would take centuries to complete and at the expense of countless peasant lives:

> I have travelled to the northern border and returned by the Direct Road. As I went along I saw the towers of the Great Wall which [General] Meng T'ien constructed for the Qin [Dynasty]. He cut through the mountains and filled up the valleys opening up a direct road. Truly he made free with the strength of the common people!

Ultimately, Watson describes the Grand Historian 'as a romantic and a conservative who, like many historians, lived in the past and could not see that the old ideals of personal freedom, the old chivalric codes of personal loyalty, could not survive in a great unified empire administered by a complex bureaucracy'.

Other than the *Shiji*, there are two further seminal texts about the predominant ethnic group of China. The first is the *Hanshu* (Book of Han) composed by Ban Gu (or Pan Ku), who also continued a text begun by his father. When the son died in prison in AD 92, it was completed a decade later by his sister Ban Zhao (China's first known female historian), some two centuries *after* the *Shiji*. It covers the Han Dynasty during its initial 200-year rule (206 BC–AD 9) before it was replaced by the Xin Dynasty for a short period, only for the Han to reassert itself for another two centuries (AD 25–220). The first half of the dynasty is therefore referred to as the Former Han, while the second half as the Later Han. Its history was continued in the *Hou Hanshu* (Book of the Later Han), compiled 300 years after the *Hanshu*.

Both these records draw substantially on the *Shiji*, in many cases almost word for word, and there are numerous parallels between them.* However, since the *Shiji* was the primary text, written soon after the first caravans began venturing west—initiating the Silk Road and its Stone Tower—it is given prominence in this book. Some Sinologists believe its key section and the one most relevant to us, concerning the Western Regions of China (Chapter 123), was in fact lost and reconstructed *later* based on the *Hanshu*; but, either way, the contents of both texts are similar. Another reason for quoting widely from the *Shiji* is to give new readers a chance to appreciate this revered text and its nuances while deciding for themselves the veracity of Sima Qian's monumental work.

---

*   In this book, all translations from the *Shiji* are by Burton Watson, from the *Hanshu* by A. F. P. Hulsewe, from the *Hou Hanshu* by John Hill.

2

Barbarians from the North

He watched his woman preparing their evening meal over the dung fire, the smoke rising through the opening in their yurt. It smelt good; hunks of fatty mutton bubbling in a stew of curdled milk, spiced with wild herbs, to be eaten with flat bread. The fat would help the children ward off the cold, which troubled his old stab wound still. She, a captured slave, had long replaced his first wife, who had not recovered from a fever that had also claimed many of the tribe. And she had already borne him two children; both had her fine features, enhanced by the mixed blood of Sogdiana and the Steppe. Now she was one of them and could ride and make kumis from mares' milk. She had also learnt the essential art of working wool into thick felt, used to line the walls of their yurt and to make clothing, saddle-pads and boot lining. But lately she had begun talking of a return south, to her land between the two rivers. Fearful, she cried, that cold or illness would claim their baby daughter or, heaven forbid, their son, who could already ride like the wind. The loss of either, he knew, would break her heart as she had little else.

From its first capital in Chang'an (meaning 'perpetual peace', modern-day Xi'an), which was one of the largest cities of the world at the time, a succession of Han emperors would send their armies northwest. They would make the long march through the Gansu Corridor—also known as the Hexi Corridor—to extend their territory into the Western Regions (today Xinjiang province).

For most of their rule, Han armies fought here to keep the northern barbarians out, in keeping with two old adages: the security of the Chinese capital is defended at its furthest frontiers; and, whosoever wishes to rule the Middle Kingdom must first hold the Gansu Corridor. The Han would add to and strengthen what would eventually become one of the wonders of our world, the Great Wall. It was started in Gansu as whitewashed rammed earthworks—quite unlike its popular modern image of imposing walls and towers made of stone, which were only built a thousand years later. Despite hundreds of thousands of soldiers being stationed along its entire length, the old wall would often prove ineffective in the Han's life-and-death struggle against these persistent marauders. Nevertheless, it at least posed a barrier of sorts to their horses, without which they were impotent and would never think of abandoning. Although the wall could be relied on to gain time for the sentries as they waited for reinforcements to arrive, this was not always enough. At one point in 166 BC, for example, a hoard of 140,000 horsemen would raid to within 300 *li* (120 kilometres) of the capital, causing widespread panic.

These raiders were the Xiongnu, but for historians they remain an elusive people particularly since, having no script of their own, they left no written records. According to historian Nicola Di Cosmo:

> After several decades of debates, questions relating to the ethnic and linguistic identity of the Xiongnu are still unanswered. Likewise, the possibility of finding in Chinese sources clues about the 'roots' of the Xiongnu phenomenon is faint at best.*

They were part of a loose group of tribes called *Saka* (or *Shaka* by Indians, *Scythian* by Greeks, *Sai* by Chinese). Their horsemen warriors reigned supreme at the time, ranging between the Caspian Sea and the Great Wall of China across what is referred to as the Eurasian Steppe

---

* The Xiongnu (Hsiung-nu) would be later identified as the Huns who threatened Europe—but academics are not in agreement about this.

Route. The Xiongnu Empire was the first of its kind to dominate these sprawling steppe lands and would also be the longest—lasting some 300 years—even becoming a prototype of sorts for other empires (including the Mongols who would follow many centuries later). Sima Qian notes in the prelude to his chapter when describing them: 'The Han has attempted to determine the Xiongnu's periods of strength and weakness so that it may adopt defensive measures or launch punitive expeditions as the circumstances allow.'

The Xiongnu would repeatedly contest a strategically significant region north of the Han capital called Ordos.* This area of roughly 1,000 square kilometres is formed by the great bend in the silt-laden Huang He (Yellow River), which large sections of the Great Wall were built to protect. Although geographically part of China, ecologically it represents the southern end of the steppe. Today, much of this region is arid, but back then it was more fertile—as was the Gansu Corridor—containing grasslands and forests.

The speed of the Xiongnu's attack, combined with expert horsemanship and archery, was legendary. They seemed to materialize out of nowhere, mounted on hardy ponies that their country was ideal for breeding. The *Shiji* provides a picture of their lifestyle:

> They move about in search of water and pasture and have no walled cities or fixed dwellings, nor do they engage in any kind of agriculture. Their lands, however, are divided into regions under the control of various leader. They have no writing, and even promises and agreements are only verbal. The little boys start out by learning to ride sheep and shoot birds and rats with a bow and arrow . . . Thus all the young men are able to use a bow and act as armed cavalry in time of war.

The women, too, were remarkable horse riders, who assisted in training their children to use the bow and were themselves fierce

---

* The northern half of Ordos sits within present-day Inner Mongolia.

fighters when defending their homes from attack. The reason for the Xiongnu's unsettled ways and constant movement in search of pastures is explained by a simple proverb from the steppe: 'Without pastures there are no herds, without herds there is no food, and without food there are no people.'

In accordance with their belief system, the tribes made sacrificial offerings to the earth, heavenly bodies, their spirits and ancestors. Their *shanyu* (or *chanyu*, meaning 'supreme leader') made Shamanism their state religion and would describe himself as 'born of heaven and earth, brought forth by the sun and moon'.

The bow that Sima Qian referred to above played a critical role in Eurasian history and is better described as the 'composite bow'. The advantage gained by the user of this weapon was *the* decisive factor in the increased military activity of the hordes and their rise to becoming steppe empires. Its secret lay in its construction: fashioned from wood, animal horn and sinew, the components were laminated together with glue from boiled hides (on the dry steppe there was little chance of the glue becoming wet and disintegrating). Although shorter in length than the later English longbow, the energy stored in the flexed horn and sinew made its firing power greater than all-wooden bows, and the arrows it discharged could even pierce armour. According to John Man, it 'ranks with the Roman sword and the machine gun as a weapon that changed the nature of warfare'.

These steppe warriors were so lethal with their bow that their preference was always to engage in battle as mounted archers; and they would rather withdraw behind a parting cloud of arrows than draw swords and fight hand-to-hand.* Indeed, the supremacy of the mounted archer was such that, even prior to the Han, Chinese armies had begun abandoning their chariots and copying the enemy's tactics, including adopting trousers by their cavalry in place of tunics, to better ride and shoot.

---

* This technique of firing arrows backwards from a horse at full gallop (without the aid of stirrups, which probably were not invented then) became known as the 'Parthian shot'.

Despite the barbarians' highly developed war machine, the Chinese looked down on these shepherds with clothes made from animal skins and a seemingly wild manner of living. Their young warriors were known to take the first pick of any food, while the old received leftovers; and on the death of their fathers the sons took their wives, except for their own mothers. Of course, the Xiongnu were particularly demonized for steadfastly refusing to accept Han superiority and pay homage to the Son of Heaven. And they were frustratingly wily opponents too, as the *Shiji* goes on to record:

> If the battle is going well for them they will advance, but if not, they will retreat, for they do not consider it a disgrace to run away. Their only concern is self-advantage, and they know nothing of propriety or righteousness.

Sima Qian also notes a description of them from another contemporary chronicler:

> It is not only our generation which finds the Xiongnu difficult to conquer and control. They make a business of pillage and plunder, and indeed this would seem their inborn nature . . . no attempt has ever been made to order or control them; rather, they have been regarded as beasts to be pastured, not as members of the human race.

This picture of the northern 'barbarians' is a bleak one and probably exaggerated since, due to their lack of literacy, their history was recorded by the vanquished rather than the victors (as would be the case with the Mongols). Moreover, the name 'Xiongnu' which the Chinese saddled them with, also underscores their disdain of these steppe dwellers, translating roughly as 'illegitimate offspring of slaves'—they, however, called themselves 'Hunnu' meaning 'People of the Sky'.

The prime reason the Xiongnu were considered barbarians was due to their ruthlessness, as the story of their Prince Modu (or Motun) demonstrates. Sima Qian relates how, although heir apparent, he was sent away by his father, the shanyu, as a hostage to their bitter rivals, the Yuezhi (or Yueh-chih). He did this to promote a younger son from a more favoured consort, attacking the Yuezhi soon afterwards with the expectation that Modu would be killed in retaliation. But, just as they were about to do so, the prince managed to steal one of their best horses and escape; impressing the shanyu, who then put him in command of 10,000 cavalry.

Modu, however, was not about to forget or forgive his father's treachery. In planning revenge, he had arrows made that whistled in flight, and drilled his archers saying: 'Shoot wherever you see my whistling arrow strike! . . . anyone who fails to shoot will be cut down!' After testing their instant obedience targeting birds and animals, he shot an arrow first into one of his best horses and then his favourite wife, immediately executing anyone who refused to follow suit. Finally, while hunting with his father, he shot an arrow into the shanyu and every one of his men did likewise. Then, after killing his younger brother and stepmother, and any high officials who refused to obey him, he conquered all the other tribal clans. Thus, he became the supreme ruler of a united Xiongnu.

Modu would be shanyu for thirty-five years (209–174 BC) and prove to be one of the most potent rulers of ancient Central Asia. He instituted laws that strengthened his hold amongst the clans; for example, evading military service or any show of indiscipline carried the death penalty. Modu reorganized his troops, replacing heavily armoured horsemen with light cavalry that was highly manoeuvrable and armed with the composite bow. Within a matter of years, he transformed a collection of steppe tribes into an empire as they reached their peak in strength and size. The Han would lose a disastrous battle against them in the eighth year of his reign and were forced to adopt a strategy of *heqin* (peace and affinity), which essentially amounted to appeasing the Xiongnu by paying large annual tributes—to save face, the Han called them 'gifts'.

After years of raiding and battling the Han, the Grand Historian tells us how Modu finally offered to make peace. He sent their emperor a camel and ten horses together with a long message, including the words:

> All the people who live by drawing the bow are now united into one family and the entire region of the north is at peace. Thus I wish now to lay down my weapons, rest my soldiers, and turn my horses to pasture . . . [that] generation after generation enjoy peace and comfort.

The emperor, keen to make a pact of brotherhood with the Xiongnu, sent many fine clothes, silks and other gifts in return, replying: 'We heartily approve of these words. This indeed is the way the sage rulers of antiquity would have spoken.' But Modu died shortly afterwards, and the peace was soon broken as his immediate successors proceeded to repeatedly attack northern China, reigniting the steppe dynamics of 'trade or raid'.

Other than paying tribute and exchanging gifts, another way of avoiding frontier conflicts was for both sides to engage in hostage swaps. Han princesses were sent across the Great Wall in marriage, while the sons of chieftains came to live in the capital. These exchanges did not always end well; as was the case following the death of a chief from the kingdom of Loulan (also known as Kroraina). The tribe now demanded the return of their young prince to take over his father's mantle but, as the *Hanshu* relates:

> [He] had been indicted according to the terms of the Han laws and sent down to the silk-worm house to undergo castration. For this reason Han did not send him to Loulan, but affirmed in reply that 'the Son of Heaven has become greatly attached to his attendant and is unable to send him

away; in his place you should enthrone the next son who is suitable to accede.'*

The people of Loulan, being less powerful, had no option but to heed their overlord's advice and appoint his brother instead.

Another example of such an exchange, also mentioned in the *Hanshu*, was the case of a Han princess being married off to a northern chief. She only saw her elderly husband once or twice a year, with neither speaking the other's tongue, prompting her song of sorrow:

> My family sent me off to be married on the other side of heaven;
> They sent me a long way to a strange land, to the king of Wusun.
> A domed lodging is my dwelling place with walls made of felt;
> Meat is my food, with fermented milk as the sauce.
> I live with constant thoughts of my home, my heart is full of sorrow;
> I wish I were a golden swan, returning to my home country.

To make matters worse, she was demoted after the more powerful Xiongnu also sent the king of Wusun a princess, who was then declared senior consort. In the second century BC, twelve Han princesses were married off to various shanyus in this way; the hope being that, as part of the 'family' now and with their offspring considered royalty, the tribes would give up their raiding south into China.

The *Shiji* records the efforts of the earlier Emperor Wen (reigned 180–157 BC) to make peace with Modu's successor, despite broken treaties in the past:

> Our two great nations, the Han and the Xiongnu, stand side by side. Since the Xiongnu dwell in the north, where the land is cold and the killing frosts come early, we have decreed that our

---

* All translations from the *Hanshu* are by A. F. P. Hulsewe.

officials shall send to the Shanyu each year a fixed quantity of millet, leaven, gold, silk, cloth, thread, floss and other articles.

Once a treaty was concluded, the emperor issued an edict:

The Xiongnu shall not enter within our borders, nor shall the Han forces venture beyond the frontier. Anyone who violates this agreement shall be executed. It is to the advantage of both nations that they should live in lasting friendship and without further aggression.

For the Xiongnu, promising peace in return for tribute would soon make up most of their revenues. But, within years, the barbarians reneged and began raiding at their pleasure, hungry for booty. Traditionally, a warrior who brought back the head of an enemy was permitted to keep all his plunder, which could include fine goods, animals and prisoners (soon to be slaves). If he happened to recover the body of a fallen comrade, he got to keep his property as well. The Han army had its own rules: one dictated that a commander's achievement was measured by subtracting his own losses from the number of enemy combatants killed. Another stipulated the death penalty for any general beaten in battle, while the family of an officer allowing himself to be taken prisoner was persecuted. Not surprisingly, such rules sometimes encouraged defeated Han generals and families to defect to the enemy instead.

Wu Di took the throne in 141 BC aged fifteen; his reign would last fifty-four years and not be eclipsed in terms of length for another 1,800 years. A man of tremendous energy, although it was sometimes misdirected, Watson's assessment of him goes on to state: 'Yet not since the First Emperor of the Qin, whom Emperor Wu at times disturbingly resembles, had China had such a vigorous and strong-willed ruler, nor was she to have another for many centuries to come.'

The Grand Historian was alive during his rule, and provides first-hand reports of an era that would mark the high point of the Former Han, and of Wu's dealings with the Xiongnu:

When the present emperor came to the throne he reaffirmed the peace alliance and treated the Xiongnu with generosity, allowing them to trade in the markets of the border stations and sending them lavish gifts. From the Shanyu on down, all the Xiongnu grew friendly with the Han, coming and going along the Great Wall.

But almost from the start, Emperor Wu wished to put an end to the passive *heqin* strategy adopted by his predecessors and free the Han permanently from Xiongnu belligerence, starting what would eventually become a two-century-long struggle with their northern neighbours.

Seven years later, in a bold and devious move, Emperor Wu set a trap for them. He sent an influential trader from one of his cities, disguised as a refugee, to carry contraband goods to the Xiongnu and begin trading with them. Then, upon winning their confidence, the trader offered to turn over the city for pillage after murdering its key officials. To set the trap, he hung the heads of some condemned criminals on the outer wall, as per the agreed signal with the Xiongnu, while 300,000 Han troops waited in a nearby valley ready to pounce.

The shanyu took the bait and crossed the border with 100,000 horsemen but became suspicious as he approached the city. The *Shiji* relates how, upon noticing that 'although the fields were full of animals, there was not a single person in sight', as a precaution he first captured a watchtower whose commander, to save his own life, divulged the Han deception. Turning around, the shanyu and his cavalry fled, and upon safely returning home he exclaimed: 'Heaven was on my side when I captured this defense official. In effect Heaven sent you to warn me!' The pages that follow in the *Shiji* are filled with descriptions of broken treaties, attacks and counter-attacks by both parties; each side committing tens of thousands of troops in numerous battles, leading to vast numbers dead or taken prisoner.

Earlier, however, within two years of taking the throne and *before* precipitating this latest war, Emperor Wu and his court had come up with a bold plan. Its underlying strategy was based on the expedient adage: *The enemy of my enemy is my friend*. The Han had learnt from captured warriors of the existence of another nomadic confederacy, the Yuezhi, who were thought to reside somewhere in the vicinity of the Western Regions. In the not-too-distant past, they had been a formidable force, but were conquered by the Xiongnu around 162 BC and forced to move west (more about their momentous migration later). Afterwards, as was customary, the victorious shanyu had fashioned the skull of their defeated king into a drinking cup. Emperor Wu was told that the Yuezhi harboured a constant grudge against their old enemy, and had previously sought alliances with other confederacies, hoping to take revenge. He therefore decided to make a pact with the Yuezhi and use them to open a second front against the Xiongnu—they could attack their mutual enemy from the west while Han armies approached from the south. To this end, he sent an envoy to seek out the Yuezhi, wherever they might be.

3

The Journey West

They had made their preparations, although there was not much to prepare as a nomad dismantles his dwelling within the hour. He had horses for each of them, a wagon to carry their yurt and few belongings, and a small flock of fat-tailed sheep making up all he owned. His people had been understanding and given them small gifts; while secretively pressing upon his woman a talisman to ward off the evil spirits that were sure to abound beyond their grasslands. Some of his fellow tribesmen had already moved south into the settlements, particularly during drought years when grazing became scarce, while others lived on the fringes, farming over summer and pasturing their herds in winter. Recently, caravans had begun passing across the steppe, coming from the direction of the morning sun. From their looks, it was evident they were Chinese, and they carried dazzling gifts and goods to trade. They were seeking out new kingdoms to the west, or so his people had learnt from the interpreters who accompanied them. Their caravans sometimes stretched out as far as the eye could see; perhaps if one was heading towards Sogdiana, his family could join it. He would seek out her people and stay if they were made welcome; or go further into the valley where he had heard there was a living to be made working with horses. One could not deny that the country there produced the best horses, but his people were undoubtedly the better horsemen.

Zhang Qian (or Chang Ch'ien) had been a court attendant and an officer of the palace guard when he answered Emperor Wu's call for a volunteer to find and engage the Yuezhi. Past the age of thirty when he set out in 139 BC, his would be one of the greatest journeys of discovery of all time.*

Figure 1. The Journey West: Emperor Wu (centre) dispatching Zhang Qian (kneeling); detail from a Tang Dynasty mural

Being the emperor's envoy, he hoisted the insignia of his imperial mission on a tall bamboo pole: three long tufts from a yak's tail (its hair being a symbol of power across much of Asia). Accompanying him were one hundred men, including a disaffected Xiongnu archer named Ganfu, who had been taken prisoner years earlier and would now act as guide and interpreter. Sima Qian would later make a full record of their epic journey and describe how they soon ran into big trouble by initially deciding to take the short route through Xiongnu territory. Upon entering it, the party was soon captured and brought before the shanyu, who protested:

> The Yuezhi people live to the north of me. What does the Han mean by trying to send an envoy to them! Do you suppose that if I tried to send an embassy to the kingdom of Yueh in the southeast the Han would let my men pass through China?

---

* The year of his birth is not known, while key dates and his exact itinerary remain uncertain.

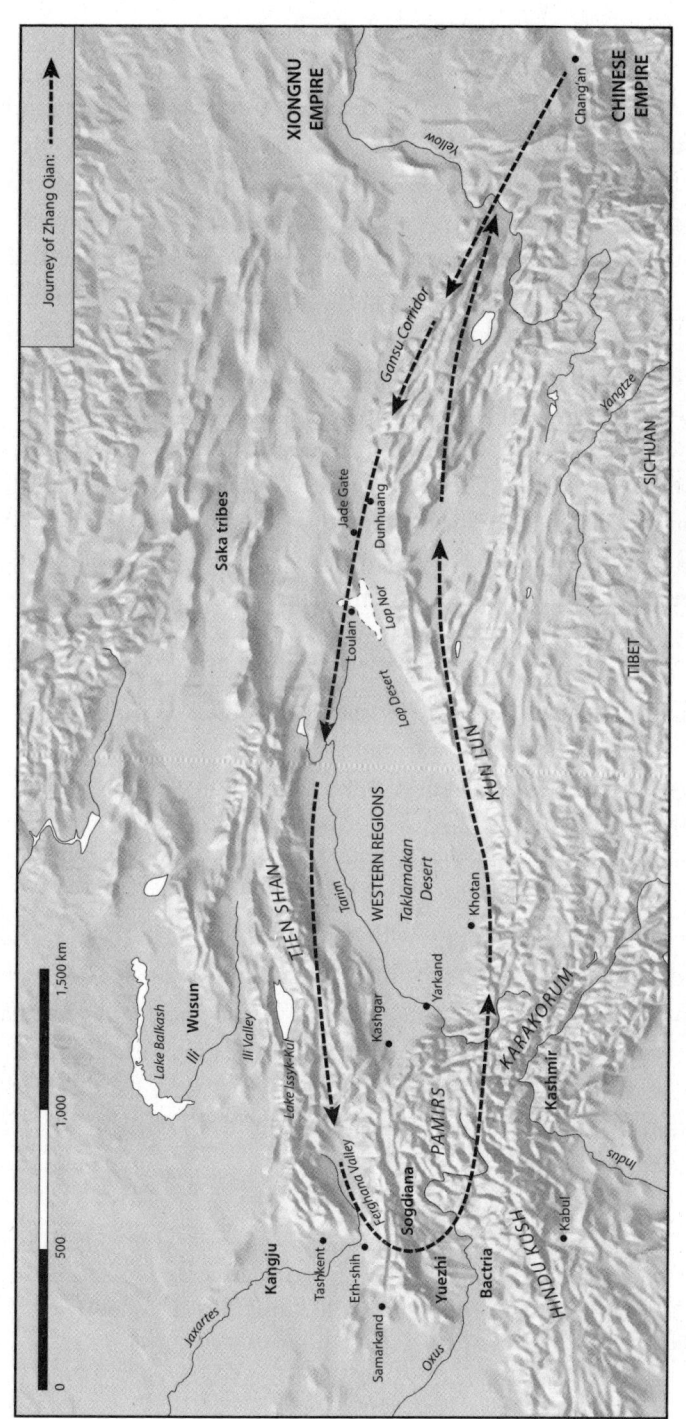

Map 2. Central Asia: marking the journey of Zhang Qian

The envoy and his men were detained for many years, but the barbarians came to love Zhang Qian and the shanyu gave him a wife from their own people, who bore him a son.* After *ten years* in captivity, he managed to escape on foot with her and some of his men. Afraid and on the run, their party suffered great hardship from which many did not survive. Rather than abandon his mission, though, Zhang Qian led this group further west to Loulan on the shores of the Lop Nor (lake). After resting, hunting, and taking on provisions here, they pushed on along the northern edge of the massive Taklamakan Desert. Further still, they passed through the kingdom of Ferghana with its population of several hundred thousand, located in the lush Ferghana Valley.† Here, they saw fine horses and alfalfa, which grows abundantly and provides excellent forage. Zhang Qian had managed to hang on to his imperial credential all this time, and upon presenting it to the king he requested his assistance:

> I was dispatched as envoy of the Han to the Yuezhi, but the Xiongnu blocked my way and I have only just managed to escape. I beg Your Highness to give me some guides to show me the way. If I can reach my destination and return to the Han to make my report, the Han will reward you with countless gifts!

Keen to establish relations with China and obtain a share of its wealth, the king of Ferghana obliged, escorting Zhang Qian's party to Kangju (or K'ang-chu, a state which probably included Sogdiana). It lay by the twin great *daryas* (rivers) of Central Asia, known to the Greeks as the Oxus and Jaxartes (today the Amu Darya and Syr Darya respectively). They, in turn, led him to the Yuezhi, who had

---

* Contrary to the *Shiji*, the *Hanshu* records 'by whom he had children', but neither mentions their fate.
† Today, this 300 km-long valley (140 km at its widest point) straddles southern Kyrgyzstan, northern Tajikistan and eastern Uzbekistan.

made their new home in Bactria (today northern Afghanistan), or Da Xia as it was known to the Chinese.

Here in 128 BC, Zhang Qian was finally presented to their supreme leader, to whom he delivered Emperor Wu's message and extended the Han's 'hand of friendship'. But the son of the previously slain ruler was not interested in avenging his father, nor participating in a joint attack on their old enemy. The Xiongnu had already bested them three times since Modu's initial attack, and thirty-four years had passed since their enforced migration had taken them across the breadth of Central Asia. Whereas here and now, after having conquered the previous inhabitants, the Yuezhi were well-settled in a rich and fertile land. They had no intention of continuing past quarrels; besides, the Han lived far away whereas the Xiongnu still roamed close by.

Despite being unable to secure an alliance, Zhang Qian spent a year exploring this region, and its legendary capital Balkh (or Bactra to the Greeks) located south of the Oxus. Besides visiting neighbouring lands, the envoy gathered information about other states in the area and heard vague reports of a whole new world lying even further to the west—countries such as Rome and Parthia (ancient Persia/Iran). Even today, his accounts remain important to historians, as they represent the first Chinese records of any region lying to the west of China.

When his time of discovery was over, Zhang Qian may have made one last attempt to convince the Yuezhi ruler but was again turned down. At which point he decided to return home, only this time by a different route skirting south of the Taklamakan Desert and along the northern edge of Tibet. But his adversaries were everywhere, and his party was once again captured by the Xiongnu, who enslaved him, although this time his detention was shorter. A year later, when the incumbent shanyu died it set off a power struggle; in the ensuing turmoil Zhang Qian escaped with his wife and Ganfu, before making a dash for home. After thirteen years, he arrived in the capital to a hero's welcome where he solemnly returned to his emperor the mission's insignia lofted on a pole. Although his undertaking to forge a pact with the Yuezhi had been unsuccessful, he was nevertheless promoted to high rank, and Ganfu was honoured as well.

Emperor Wu—and presumably with him, Sima Qian too—listened attentively to his envoy's extraordinary report, describing all he had seen, the people encountered along the way, and the goods they had to offer. In Ferghana, for example, he saw wine produced from grapes and brought back its seed—resulting in the grapevine becoming one of China's classic imports courtesy of the Silk Road. Zhang Qian also related an incredible sight he had witnessed there in the valley: a superb breed of horses that seemed to sweat blood. (In fact, the bleeding was caused from lesions inflicted by a parasite on the back and shoulders of the horses, which would then swell and burst.) A mixture of history and legend about the origin of these animals recounts:

> In the country of Ferghana there are high mountains. There are horses there which cannot be captured. Leopard-spotted mares are released at the foot of the mountains so that they might couple with these horses. The foals which result sweat blood, which is why they are said to be of the race of the celestial horses.

This last piece of information gained Emperor Wu's complete attention, and in more ways than one, as we shall see.

The emperor was particularly pleased to hear that all the great states visited by his envoy thought highly of Han goods and wealth; and to learn that although they, too, were home to settled people, they were militarily weak. This presented Wu Di an opportunity to greatly expand his empire, as the *Shiji* relates, and 'attract to his court men of strange customs . . . and his might would come to be known to all the lands within the four seas'. The difficulty, however, lay in getting past the hostile Xiongnu, as his envoy had found out from years in captivity. Yet Zhang Qian thought there may be a way around this, as he outlined to his emperor:

When I was in Bactria, I saw bamboo canes in Ch'iung and cloth made in the province of Shu [both in Sichuan, then not a part of China]. When I asked the people how they had gotten such articles, they replied, 'Our merchants go to buy them in the markets of Shentu [India]' . . . The region is said to be hot and damp. The inhabitants ride elephants when they go into battle. The kingdom is situated on a great river.

By calculating distances and directions from China to Bactria and northern India, Zhang Qian realized the following:

If we could find a new route from Shu via the land of Shentu, however, we would have a short and convenient way to reach Ferghana which would avoid the danger of the northern route!

His mention of Shentu was the first reliable report of India ever received by Chinese authorities. Sometime earlier, though, the Han had tried to establish relations with the people from Shu, whom they labelled 'southwestern barbarians', but without success as no viable road could be found. Now the emperor was keen to try again and ordered his envoy to find a route from Shu to Bactria, altogether bypassing the Xiongnu.*

The expedition, comprising four separate groups, started out from different points, but ultimately all were unsuccessful. They were blocked by small, hostile tribes who seized and even murdered some of the Han envoys. But the overall knowledge gained from this mission would encourage Emperor Wu to redouble his efforts in establishing relations with the tribes to the southwest. Finding this route inaccessible also gave the Han more impetus to stabilize the primary route through the Western Regions, and deal with the northern barbarians once and for all.

---

* This route went via present-day Myanmar and Bangladesh, then up the Ganges River into Afghanistan.

On his return, Zhang Qian was appointed a subordinate commander and accompanied the Han army against the Xiongnu. During this deployment, he gained distinction through his prior knowledge of enemy territory by locating water and pasturage, thereby preventing suffering for soldiers and animals alike. For his efforts, he was invested with the title Po-wang or 'Broad Vision' marquis.

The following year in 122 BC, Zhang Qian was appointed Colonel of the Guard and dispatched in support of another army on a further engagement with the Xiongnu. But this time disaster struck: the Han army was surrounded and suffered heavy losses. Zhang Qian was blamed for the defeat after his column arrived late for a rendezvous with the main army. For this lapse he was sentenced to death but escaped the ultimate punishment by purchasing a pardon (which Sima Qian was unable to do) and being reduced to the status of a commoner.

However, after a time, Zhang Qian was able to regain his appointment as envoy, this time to engage with the Wusun. They were a semi-nomadic, pastoral nation who, after defeating the Yuezhi fifteen years earlier, had replaced them along the Ili River. Their country lay between the two large lakes of Balkash and Issyk-Kul, where they had built a walled capital. The way in which Zhang Qian broached this subject not only illustrates how he managed to reverse his demotion, but also shows his acumen: Emperor Wu would occasionally question him about the Western Regions and their 'uncivilized' people; so he related the story of the Wusun and how they had become more powerful, following years of alliance with the Xiongnu. Recently, they had ceased to obey them and successfully resisted their attempts to be subjugated further. Zhang Qian then put forward his strategy:

> The barbarians are well known to be greedy for Han wealth and goods. If we could make use of this opportunity to send rich gifts and bribes to the Wusun people and persuade them

to move farther east and occupy the region which formerly belonged to Kunmo*, then the Han could conclude an alliance of brotherhood with them . . . If we could get them to obey us, it would be like cutting off the right arm of the Xiongnu!

He also pointed out that if the Wusun became their allies 'Bactria and the other countries to the west could all be persuaded to come to court and acknowledge themselves our foreign vassals'. Emperor Wu was convinced, and promptly appointed Zhang Qian as a general of palace attendants. Thus, some twenty years after his first expedition, the envoy left on a final mission with a 300-strong force, each man taking two horses. Many deputies accompanied him in the hope that the roads would be passable, allowing them to visit neighbouring states. To this end, the delegation 'took along tens of thousands of cattle and sheep and carried gold and silk goods worth a hundred billion cash'. Although the value stated in the *Shiji* is obviously metaphorical, it represents the first historical record of large-scale export of silk from China.

When the Han envoys presented themselves in the Wusun court, their king named Kunmo (or K'un-mo) attempted to treat them as he had been treated by the Xiongnu. Zhang Qian was outraged and, knowing him to be greedy, exclaimed: 'The Son of Heaven has sent me with these gifts, but if you do not prostrate yourself to receive them, I shall have to take them back!' Kunmo did so immediately in order to accept the gifts, whereupon the envoy delivered the message from his emperor: 'If the Wusun will consent to move east . . . then the Han will send you a princess of the imperial family to be your wife.'

The Wusun, however, were no longer united as they had been in the past, and Kunmo was old now. His ministers, afraid of the Xiongnu, did not want to return; while he did not dare to make

---

* Although the *Shiji* uses 'the Hun-yeh king', Hulsewe believes this should read 'Kunmo'.

promises for all the tribes, nor commit to a pact. Instead, he provided Zhang Qian's deputies with guides and interpreters to allow them to visit other states including Ferghana, Sogdiana, and even further afield to India and Parthia.

Meanwhile, Zhang Qian returned home accompanied by many Wusun ambassadors, who brought with them thirty of their best horses as a gift for Emperor Wu.* The barbarians were now able to see for themselves the extent and greatness of the Han empire. Subsequently, in exchange for a thousand horses, the Wusun forged a matrimonial alliance with the Han. The princess involved in this case was the one referred to earlier, and on hearing her song of sorrow. Emperor Wu sent gifts of embroideries and brocades every other year. (Her husband Kunmo, being too old, later gave her away in marriage to his grandson.)

Following this successful mission, Zhang Qian was honoured by his emperor and promoted to the position of Grand Messenger, making him one of nine highest-ranked ministers of state. He died in office a year later in 113 BC, aged about sixty; his grave lies in his home town southwest of Chang'an.†

Zhang Qian's expedition reports were instrumental in persuading Emperor Wu to adopt an expansionist policy that would soon lead to a greatly expanded Han 'tributary' empire. His deputies began returning home a year after his death; and in many cases they, too, brought back ambassadors from the lands they visited. In this way, China made contact with faraway nations for the first time, and began establishing relationships that would last for centuries; the Grand Historian duly recorded:

> Zhang Qian was a man of great strength, determination, and generosity. He trusted others and in turn was liked by the

---

* Initially, Emperor Wu called them Heavenly Horses, but later reserved this term for the blood-sweating ones from Ferghana.

† Some historians believe he died six years earlier, while others place it a decade later. During repairs to his tomb in 1945, a clay mould was found inscribed 'Home of the Po-wang', recalling his title as marquis.

barbarians . . . [He] opened the way . . . and all the envoys who journeyed to the lands in later times relied upon his reputation to gain them a hearing. As a result, the foreign states trusted the Han envoys.

Justly credited for opening up the road west, he remains a national hero of China, and is considered the Father of the Silk Road. Historian Craig Benjamin adds: 'It is no exaggeration to suggest that the expedition of Zhang Qian changed the course of world history.'

4

Heavenly Horses

The horses were magnificent beasts, strong and spirited, even better than the stories told of them back home. Some said they were from heaven— the finest amongst them certainly looked it. To see them at full gallop along the lush grasslands as the sun rose was a sight to behold. Although the best of them were untouchable and forbidden to the likes of him, he sought out the herd on many a morning just to be in their presence as they thundered past. He had felt the resentment from her people when his family had first arrived unannounced, and they looked down on his half-blood children. So, they had moved on, and he eventually found work in the valley doing what came easily to him, looking after the regular horses. His days were long and busy: breeding foals, breaking in the young mounts, finding the best pasture, adding alfalfa to their feed, and always running the herd hard to build up its strength and stamina. The handlers who worked with him saw how he loved these horses; but the foreigners from the east coveted them too and picked out the best ones. Although they were always ready to pay his master more than a fair price, he could not help wondering if one day they would be used as cavalry against his own people.

Emperor Wu was much taken by Zhang Qian's initial report about the mysterious and high-spirited horses he had seen in Ferghana, for two quite different reasons: the first being his fascination with immortality; and the second, his country's desperate need to continually strengthen its cavalry and match the mounted Xiongnu in battle. So grim was the Han's stock in horses, it is said that their first emperor was unable to find four horses of the same colour in all his realm to pull his chariot.

A land of agriculturists, China has always had difficulty breeding horses; and according to Austin Coates, who wrote a history about horse racing there, this is 'due to the calcium deficiency in all [their] organic matter and water'.* Furthermore, historian Gerald Morgan points out:

> As the horse can only breed and flourish between certain latitudes, the axis of movement was bound to be eastwards and westwards and, as a map of vegetation will show, the great steppe-grazing regions extend from Mongolia westwards into Europe rather than eastwards into China.

Due to this inherent disadvantage, the Han resorted to importing hardy Mongolian ponies, which the steppe tribes bred so successfully and had used with such devastating effectiveness against them. Tens of thousands would be required every year just to replace their mounts fallen in multiple battles. They would also introduce donkeys into China, buying them from the Wusun in large numbers—other than being impressed with their work rate, they found them easier to breed.

As to his first interest, the emperor was not alone in believing infinite longevity to be a right of the Son of Heaven. The first emperor to unify the country and give shape to the Great Wall had also thought it so and had fervently sought the elixir of life. Although his rule was short-lived, being replaced fifteen years later by the Han Dynasty, Emperor Qin (or Ch'in) did achieve immortality in a way,

---

* Jasper Becker writes that 'Chinese soil lacks selenium, a mineral essential for the breeding of sturdy horses'.

by giving China its Western language name.* His tomb, uncovered through sheer chance in 1974 by a group of farmers digging a well, now brings him fame too. The mausoleum complex is thought to sprawl almost 100 square kilometres and reportedly took some forty years and 700,000 peasants to complete (although these figures may be exaggerated). To keep the location of the tomb secret, many thousands of the builders and associated officials were buried alive. Today, this find represents one of the most important archaeological discoveries ever made and will take the lifetimes of many teams of archaeologists to fully investigate. It has already produced the breathtaking Terracotta Army: over 8,000 life-size warriors with horses and chariots to carry the emperor into the afterlife and protect him there.

Similarly, Emperor Wu needed to be transported when the time came. Earlier, he had consulted an oracle text *I Ching* (Book of Changes) which foretold that 'divine horses are due to appear from the northwest'. His excitement, as these long-awaited steeds from Ferghana were to finally arrive in the capital, is evident from a historically important hymn composed in 101 BC, possibly by the emperor himself:

> The Heavenly Horses are coming,
> Coming from the Far West.
> They crossed the Flowing Sands,
> For the barbarians are conquered.
> The Heavenly Horses are coming
> That issued from the waters of a pool.
> Two of them have tiger backs:
> They can transform themselves like spirits.
> The Heavenly Horses are coming
> Across the pastureless wilds

---

* This derivation is not certain, and some scholars think it may have come from Sanskrit.

A thousand leagues at a stretch,
Following the eastern road.
The Heavenly Horses are coming;
Jupiter is in the Dragon.
Should they choose to soar aloft,
Who could keep pace with them?
The Heavenly Horses are coming;
Open the gates while there is time.
They will draw me up and carry me
To the Holy Mountain of Kunlun.
The Heavenly Horses have come
And Dragon will follow in their wake.
I shall reach the Gates of Heaven,
I shall see the Palace of God.

This hymn reveals the emperor's motivation, as pointed out by renowned Sinologist Arthur Waley who translated it for his article *The Heavenly Horses of Ferghana*. He makes the distinction between the two types of horses that Emperor Wu sought: the few divine ones to satisfy his spiritual needs; and the many sturdier mounts required to continuously replenish and build up his cavalry.

Decades earlier, a minister of an earlier emperor, Wen Di, in a report titled *Guard the Frontiers and Protect the Borders*, had argued that to counter the Xiongnu, the Han military apparatus needed to be transformed from being infantry-based to cavalry-led. Many horses would be needed to bring about this policy shift, which the next emperor, Jing Di, began by instituting an equine breeding programme. By the time Wu Di succeeded him, he had approximately 450,000 military horses at his disposal.

With the ability to now confront the northern barbarians, the Martial Emperor—as Wu Di became known as—began massive and sustained attacks against them, from 119 to 105 BC, marking 'some of the largest campaigns ever seen in world history to this point' according to Craig Benjamin. Han cavalry would pursue and defeat the Xiongnu over the coming years, killing tens of thousands and taking many more prisoner, forcing the shanyu and his tribes to retreat further and further north. But the criticality of the warhorse was again demonstrated when the Han were unable to press home their advantage, after losing over 100,000 mounts during these campaigns.

Mongolian ponies are stocky, small horses, with large heads and further distinguishable by their shaggy manes and coats which grow long in winter. More importantly, they have hooves that wear down quickly, making them unsuited for long journeys or mountainous terrain if they go unshod, as was the case during that era.* Therefore, during military operations, they needed longer rest periods to allow their feet to recover, which necessitated larger herds, resulting in higher effort and cost. In contrast, the mountain-bred horses from Ferghana had harder hooves that were less susceptible to wear and tear. Allowed to run free on the grasslands, they were stronger and faster compared to Chinese horses, which were reared in stables and hand-fed fodder. Being larger too, these new horses were more capable of carrying armour-clad men and had great staying power—as the hymn alluded to earlier, they were sometimes called Thousand League horses. Finally, they possessed one other feature which made them highly prized: they were particularly handsome beasts, and their beautiful coats and sharp ears gave them a superior look.

China desperately needed better horses, because a swift cavalry with its element of surprise was the supreme weapon of war at the time. (Just as Napoleon's dictum would later equate military strength with not only an army's size, but also its speed.) In addition to their regular ponies, the Xiongnu had these superior chargers, which formed the nucleus of their prime cavalry. The Han would go to great lengths to procure horses to match them.

---

* In Europe, for example, horseshoeing only became a mainstream practice around AD 1000.

Heavenly Horses

The *Shiji* devotes a chapter to The Account of Da Yuan* [Ferghana], and describes how Emperor Wu set about obtaining this new breed of horses from its capital Erh-shih† following a report from his envoys:

> 'Ferghana has some fine horses in the city of Erh-shih, but the people keep them hidden and refuse to give any to the Han envoys!' The emperor had already taken a great liking to the horses of Ferghana, and when he heard of this he was filled with excitement and expectation. He dispatched a party of able young men and carriage masters with a thousand pieces of gold and a golden horse to go to the king of Ferghana and ask him for some the fine horses of Erh-shih.

But the king and his nobles would not part with them; and they believed China was too far away to threaten them:

> 'Furthermore, the horses of Erh-shih are one of the most valuable treasures of our state!' In the end, therefore, they refused to give the Han envoys any horses. Enraged, the Han envoys cursed the men of Ferghana, smashed the golden horse with a mallet, and departed.

The court nobles of Ferghana were furious at this wanton display, and at being treated with 'the utmost contempt'. In retaliation they arranged for another people, the Yu-ch'eng, who lived to the east of their kingdom, to kill the Han envoys as they returned to China. On learning of their death, Emperor Wu flew into a rage, initiating the so-called War of the Heavenly Horses in 104 BC.

---

* Also written as Dayuan, Ta Yuan or Ta-yuan. 'Da' or 'Ta' translates as 'great' in Chinese.
† Probably located between present-day Khujand and Samarkand.

To lead this campaign to extract both revenge and horses, while at the same time wishing to promote a relative of his favourite concubine Lady Li, the emperor chose her brother for the task. General Li Guangli (or Li Kuang-li) left the capital at the head of 6,000 regular cavalry, supported by up to 30,000 'men of bad reputation' (using criminals and undesirables in this way was common practice then, but it often led to desertions). His army soon came up against a critical problem which all columns moving through the Western Regions would face: that of securing adequate food and supplies from a sparsely populated and arid country. The inhabitants would simply barricade themselves within their walled cities and refuse to trade. Attacks by the army were sometimes successful in obtaining provisions by force, but if the city managed to hold out for more than a few days, the army moved on empty-handed. By the time General Li reached the eastern border of Ferghana ready to attack the city of Yu-ch'eng, his army was reduced to a few thousand exhausted and hungry soldiers, who were then soundly beaten with many of their number killed. Taking stock, the general and his officers realized that if they could not overcome Yu-ch'eng, then there was little chance of victory against Erh-shih.

Thus, two years after first setting out, the army retreated, but with only a fraction of their original number surviving. Just before the frontier commandery of Dunhuang (or Tun-huang) they halted at the Jade Gate, which Emperor Wu had erected and later became named for the jade-laden caravans entering from the city of Khotan (or Hotan). It allowed access through the Great Wall into China proper, and from this barrier the general sent word to his emperor explaining why he had been unable to mount an attack on Erh-shih. Not through a lack of courage, he protested, but rather from the depletion of his forces through hunger. He suggested his army be disbanded and another attempt considered at some later date. But, as the Grand Historian relates, Emperor Wu 'was enraged and sent an envoy with orders to close the pass at Jade Gate, saying that anyone from General Li's army who attempted to enter the country would be cut down on the spot'.

Figure 2. Remains of the Jade Gate, as seen by author in 2005

Meanwhile, another Han army had suffered defeat at the hands of the Xiongnu with over 20,000 soldiers being captured. The high ministers, wanting to focus their resources on avenging this defeat first, agreed with General Li and advised their emperor accordingly. Emperor Wu, however, would not be dissuaded, 'afraid that if his armies could not conquer even a small state like Ferghana, then Bactria and the other lands would come to despise the Han. No more fine horses could ever be obtained from Ferghana . . . and China would become a laughingstock among foreign nations.'

Instead, the emperor set about assembling a formidable force to reinforce his returned army, who remained camped out by the Jade Gate. He appointed fifty subordinate commanders with 60,000 new men and weapons, including freeing skilled bowmen from prison whom he armed with crossbows. The new army took with it 100,000 oxen and over 30,000 horses, as well as tens of thousands of baggage animals in the way of camels, mules, and donkeys. Additionally, 180,000 conscripts were called up for garrison and agricultural duties along the Gansu Corridor.* Officials and merchants from across the

---

* Emperor Wu had a million-strong (unpaid) conscript army, and access to around 12 million men for forced labour from some 60 million subjects.

empire were engaged in supplying dried boiled rice for the forces. Knowing that Erh-shih's inhabitants relied on water from nearby streams rather than wells, engineers were enlisted to accompany the army and divert its waterways once the city was besieged. And last but certainly not least, in anticipation of victory, two men skilled at judging horses were sent with the army, tasked with selecting Ferghana's finest to be brought back for the emperor. Sima Qian noted how: 'The whole empire was thrown into a turmoil, relaying orders and providing men and supplies for the attack on Ferghana.'

Two years after his first failed attempt, General Li set off again, but with an altogether larger force. His armed column and wagon train stretched from the Han capital 'without a break all the way west to Dunhuang'. This time, inhabitants from previously hostile settlements along the way knew better than to resist, greeting the army with gifts of food instead. In the one city that did refuse to comply, all the inhabitants were massacred after it was overcome—no other resistance was met with until Erh-shih. On the way, the army had wanted to settle their old score with Yu-ch'eng, but General Li would not be delayed, nor give the capital more time to prepare its defences. Once there, his engineers broke through the banks of the river to deny the city water, which led to extreme hardships for its inhabitants. During the next forty days, his soldiers tore down the outer wall and captured one of Erh-shih's bravest leaders, at which point the other nobles plotted against their own king:

> The reason the Han has sent troops to attack us is simply that our king Wu-kua hid his best horses and killed the Han envoys. Now if we kill the king and hand over the horses, the Han troops will most likely withdraw. Should they refuse, that will be the time to fight to the death for our city!

The king was subsequently assassinated, and his head sent to General Li with a request that troops be withdrawn. If he agreed, they would let him take his pick from Ferghana's finest, otherwise they would slaughter them rather than give the horses up. They pointed out that if it came to an all-out fight, their neighbours from Sogdiana would come to their aid, which General Li believed to be true. He had also learnt that the city had acquired the services of a Chinese who knew how to dig wells to alleviate its water shortage, and that the inhabitants still had plenty of food stored. Since his emperor's directive had been only to punish the king and bring back fine horses, the general accepted their terms of surrender.

Up to thirty of the best horses were then selected by the skilled judges. As well as 'sweating blood', two of these Heavenly Horses had stripy backs (as the earlier hymn described), which were believed to be marks from heaven and made them particularly sacred. Other than the prized steeds, over 3,000 regular stallions and mares were also chosen. Finally, after installing a new king 'who had treated the earlier Han envoys with kindness', the army began its long march home.

On the way back, the rulers of smaller states, upon hearing of the outcome in Ferghana and witnessing the might of the emperor's army, sent tributary gifts and their sons or brothers as hostages to the Han court. By the time General Li's army returned to the Jade Gate, however, its numbers had been depleted to just over 10,000 soldiers and 1,000 cavalry horses. Many men had been lost through death or desertion due to their officers 'being a greedy lot, most of them taking little care of their men but abusing and preying on them instead'. Emperor Wu, taking into account that the campaign had lasted four years, chose to overlook these losses and made General Li a marquis—he had, after all, brought back those Heavenly Horses. (A decade later, after being defeated by the Xiongnu, the general surrendered and was executed by the shanyu.)

Emperor Wu now set about rebuilding his cavalry, which was in a perilous state, having lost over 100,000 horses during campaigns against the Xiongnu (which Zhang Qian had participated in). To build a strong cavalry, three key components were necessary: acquiring better warhorses, instituting a breeding programme, and growing alfalfa as fodder.* The first would be accomplished by sourcing

---

* Also known as lucerne, alfalfa is a perennial flowering plant of the legume family.

stallions and mares from the Western Regions, by trade, by treaty, or by force. Sima Qian tells us how the Han 'sent a constant stream of envoys' to Ferghana, to the land where 'people love their wine and the horses love their alfalfa'. They offered much gold and silk to secure both the Heavenly Horses and many regular ones, together with alfalfa plants. The Han emperor also made requests to the Wusun, who sent him 1,000 horses on two occasions (and a request for a matrimonial alliance, as mentioned earlier). He established imperial stables and encouraged his nobles to set up stud farms by fixing high prices for foals, while a good mount fetched almost 150 kilograms in gold. Another contemporary record describes 300,000 horses being reared in thirty-six ranches across the Gansu Corridor and fed on the alfalfa grown there.

Within a matter of years, the horses from Ferghana became the prime warhorses of the Han, which they put to good use to dominate and expand the Middle Kingdom as a Tang Dynasty (AD 618–907) poet relates: 'The House of Han lit the beacons of war, and still the beacons blaze.' Even after the Tang, future dynasties would continue to struggle with this age-old problem, as the words of a Song Dynasty chronicler centuries later indicate:

> China has few horses, and its men are not accustomed to riding; this is our weakness . . . The court constantly tries, with our weakness, to oppose our enemies' strength, hence we lose every battle . . . Those who propose remedies for this situation merely wish to increase our armed forces in order to overwhelm the enemy. They do not realize that, without horses, we can never create an effective military force.

Despite the high value placed on steeds from Ferghana, according to horse geneticists, today their descendants have not survived in China. Yet their beauty has—a fact plainly evident by comparing depictions of the horse in Chinese art before and after the appearance of these Heavenly Horses.

Figure 3. Heavenly Horse: bronze statuette from Later Han period

5

The First Caravans

Following Zhang Qian's epic first mission, the Han began sending out more envoys to engage with newly found nations to the west. Other than goods to trade, they took expensive gifts for the nobles and their courts, an armed escort for protection, servants, and ample supplies. For such long and arduous overland journeys, they would need caravans.

They wanted him to go back with them; to look after the horses they said—too many were not surviving the crossing back east to their capital. But that place was many months away, or so he had heard. First to the end of the valley where the caravans met at the base of a holy mountain, then over cold and high passes before moving along the edges of a hot and terrible desert. He would not go that far, as returning on his own through a country he barely knew would simply be too dangerous. Whereas he would consider herding the horses as far as the mountains, if they made it worth his while. Then, before making his way back home, he could go further north and visit his people. For some years now, the frontier had been calmer, as more tribes were choosing to move south and settle down. The old feuding with the Sogdians was easing—they were a cultured people who would rather trade than fight or bear needless grudges. The thought of accompanying the caravan pleased him, especially riding with his beloved horses. Perhaps he could be of some use to the caravan leader, too, since he already knew parts of the road, as well as the ill-tempered steppe tribes they might run into. And maybe if he made the journey again sometime, his son could ride with him.

The first caravans were sent out by Emperor Wu himself and must have been elaborate affairs. Other than Ferghana, they visited many states large and small, including Bactria, India, and even travelled all the way to Parthia. The initial exchange of gifts with kingdoms would later turn into tributes—either tokens of friendship or vassalage, depending on the power structure in place. Once relationships were firmly established, this exchange would develop into regular trade, and enable the all-important taxes that flowed into state coffers from such trade. The *Shiji* describes the extent of this operation:

> The largest of these embassies to foreign states numbered several hundred persons, while even the smaller parties included over a hundred members . . . In the course of one year anywhere from five or six to over ten parties would be sent out. Those travelling to distant lands required eight or nine years to complete their journey, while those visiting nearer regions would return after a few years.

At times, these missions were so large and frequent that, as the *Hanshu* notes: 'These envoys were in sight of each other on the roads.' The taxes generated from these caravans would provide the Han Dynasty with up to thirty per cent of its cash revenues—which explains why successive Chinese rulers would make such large investments developing overland routes, while protecting caravans from harassment by belligerent tribes and bandits.

The key to controlling the route west was the Gansu Corridor, a 1,200 kilometre passageway that constricts to 15 kilometres at its narrowest point and extends northwest from the first Han capital at Chang'an. Opening into the Western Regions and its settlements around the Tarim Basin, the corridor lies sandwiched between the

Gobi Desert and the Qilian Mountains.* In the decades following Zhang Qian's return, the Han would subjugate Gansu and the Western Regions, before populating these new territories with up to two million of its own settlers, roughly equal to the entire Xiongnu nation.

Water is the critical element throughout this vast and arid region. The ability to find, store and utilize water was the overriding concern for not only the caravans, but nomadic herders and peasant settlers alike. For large expeditions, securing adequate supplies posed another major challenge since much of the area was sparsely populated. Local settlements, typically built within small oases, simply could not support a large influx of travellers and their animals. Armies, for example, had to take their own herds of cattle and carry sufficient grain to last them many months—as General Li's forces had done, having learnt from their first failed campaign.

As the Western Regions was opened up and colonized, other than strengthening the Great Wall, the emperor built four commanderies along Gansu in an effort to secure this indispensable corridor. Each one had a permanent military garrison, whose numbers were bolstered by low-ranking officials, various merchants, and by deporting 'undesirables' there. The latter—convicts and exiles—were put to work on garrison farms that were essential to keeping the settlements fed. The forts were linked by hundreds of watchtowers spaced a few kilometres apart depending on the topography, and more were built as territory extended westwards.

The expansion into the Tarim came at considerable cost to the Han economy, but a show of force was always necessary to ensure local tribes maintained loyalty to the emperor rather than turn to the Xiongnu. Eventually in 59 BC, the Western Regions was formally established as a new territory, initially comprising thirty-

---

* Once known as the Richthofen Range after the man who gave the Silk Road its name, the Qilian Mountains represent the northern outlier of the Kunlun Mountains.

six settlements. These would include cities with populations in the tens of thousands, such as Kucha, Kashgar, Yarkand and Khotan. The high office of Protector General of the Western Regions was set up and stationed east of Kucha, with a military commander duly appointed, of whom the *Hanshu* had the following to say: 'If the situation was suitable for peaceful settlement, he settled it peacefully; if it was suitable for launching an attack, he attacked.'

Going further west, the fort at Dunhuang represented the last Han outpost. Beyond this stood two *guans* (frontier passes) which allowed passage through the Great Wall, the Yang Guan and Yumen Guan (Jade Gate). They were considered the last vestiges of civilization by the Chinese, as an age-old poem warning travellers suggests:

I implore you to drink another glass of wine,
As west of the Yang Pass, no friends are to be found.

Just before Dunhuang, at the city of Anxi, the Chinese portion of the Silk Road split into two, a northern and southern arm. (In fact, there was also a 'middle arm', a shortcut of sorts, which ran from Dunhuang through to Loulan before connecting onto the northern arm. It traversed the Lop Desert but was abandoned around AD 330, probably after Loulan ran out of water when the Tarim River changed its course.) Initially, the southern arm was the more prominent route. Other than leading to the jade-bearing rivers near Khotan, further on, a route branched south at Yarkand, threading its way down into the Karakoram Mountains. Taking this trail, caravans reached the plains of India and its seaports to link with the maritime portion of the Silk Road, the so-called Spice Route. The southern arm of the Silk Road thus developed as a direct result of the growing relations between China and India.

Together with the northern arm, both trails encircled the massive Tarim Basin which stetches across some 1,600 kilometres. It covers almost a million square kilometres yet is far removed from the moderating climatic effects of any ocean. Although this basin is formed by receiving glacier-fed rivers—but which have no outlet, not even to an inland sea—it sits around 1,000 metres above sea level. Paradoxically, on its eastern edge lies the Turpan Depression, which in terms of its elevation *below* sea level is second only to the Dead Sea and its surrounds.

Dominating the Tarim's centre, where the river waters eventually evaporate or simply disappear into the sand, is one of the harshest places on the planet, the Taklamakan Desert. One translation of its name bluntly suggests: *None who enter, return*. With dunes that rise up to 300 metres, over the centuries these shifting sands of the Taklamakan (the Chinese referred to them as *Liu Sha* or 'Moving Sands') have swallowed up hundreds of towns and settlements. A few have been recently rediscovered by archaeologists, but many others still lie waiting to be uncovered.

The desert's oval shape stretches some 1,000 kilometres across and 400 kilometres north to south, making it almost the size of present-day Germany. It is hemmed in on three sides by some of the highest mountain ranges in the world, and on the fourth by another fierce desert, the Gobi. Temperatures in the Taklamakan can range in the extreme between night and day, and between winter and summer. The air here is often filled by a haze of *loess*—dust particles so fine they remain suspended for long periods, reducing visibility and disorienting travellers. A fearful area, it is desperately dry and swept by massive sandstorms. Xuanzang (or Hsuan-tsang), the celebrated Chinese monk and traveller of the seventh century, described his experience in this desert in his book *Xiyuji* (*Records of the Western Regions*):

> When these winds rise, both man and beast become confused and forgetful, and there they remain perfectly disabled. At times, sad and plaintive notes are heard and piteous cries, so that between the sights and sounds of the desert, men get confused and know not whither they go. Hence there are so

many who perish on the journey. But it is all the work of demons and evil spirits.

As camp was set up after a day's march, the caravan leader would mark the direction of travel with an arrow, since winds could obliterate their tracks overnight—without visible landmarks, they risked becoming disoriented when starting out the next morning. Yet despite their best efforts, as caravans began making their way west along the necklace of oases encircling the desert, the trails were said to be well marked by the bones of travellers and their animals who perished before reaching the mountains.

If, to escape the heat of the day, caravans travelled after sundown, this posed its own hazards and the demons of the desert remained active, as the legendary Venetian traveller Marco Polo narrated in the thirteenth century:

> [When] travellers are on the move by night, and one of them chances to lag behind or to fall asleep or the like, when he tries to gain his company again he will hear spirits talking, and will suppose them to be his comrades. Sometimes the spirits will call him by name; and thus shall a traveller ofttimes be led astray so that he never finds his party. And in this way many have perished.*

Although it is doubtful that spirits were to blame, travellers knew to be wary of the mirages which the shimmering desert conjures up, enticing caravans into its depths. As a precaution, while skirting its edges they would tie bells around the necks of their animals, and always remain close together. The playwright and poet James Elroy Flecker famously captured this image and the mood of a caravan setting out in the cool of the night:

---

* All translations from Marco Polo's accounts are by Henry Yule.

> Sweet to ride forth at evening from the wells,
> When shadows pass gigantic on the sand,
> And softly through the silence beat the bells,
> Along the Golden Road to Samarkand.

Beyond Kashgar (or Kashi), where the northern and southern arms reunited at the western edge of the Tarim, the road continued west to cross China's border and enter the famed Pamir Mountains. With peaks towering over 7,000 metres, this range is known locally as Bam-i-dunya (Roof of the World), although the *Hanshu* refers to it as Ts'ung-ling (Onion Range) because of the wild onions alleged to be growing there. The word *pamir* in fact refers to a valley plain surrounded by high mountains, and around ten separate pamirs make up this imposing range. Some of the snow falling on its slopes never melts, instead accumulating over time to form the largest ice cap on the planet outside of the polar circles. Much of this ice is trapped in a number of large glacier systems including the longest, the Fedchenko Glacier, which stretches some seventy-seven kilometres. Many of the *passes* in the Pamirs are higher than the tallest peaks in most nations and even its valleys average around 4,000 metres above sea level. In his *Geographia*, Ptolemy included the Pamirs in the mountainous divide he labelled the Imaon range, which separated his known world from that which was unknown. Although these mountains can be crossed, they have always posed a great barrier to caravans, as described in Marco Polo's account:

> The plain is called *Pamir*, and you ride across it for twelve days together, finding nothing but a desert without habitations or any green thing, so that travellers are obliged to carry with them whatever they have need of. The region is so lofty and cold that you could not even see any birds flying. And I must notice also that because of this great cold, fire does not burn so brightly, nor give out so much heat as usual, nor does it cook food so effectually.

If the harsh geography and climate did not claim the caravans, there was every chance that hostile tribes or bandits would, as the goods they transported made them obvious targets (early on, silk was worth its weight in gold). Envoys took large quantities of valuable items, as gifts or tribute to suitably impress other kingdoms. Merchants preferred to carry small, non-perishable goods that (hopefully) would be in great demand and fetch high prices in the courts of nobles or in the bazaars.

While the caravanners had no intention of antagonizing the tribesmen whose lands they passed through, many locals saw them as intruders who drew water from their wells and impinged on their grazing lands—there was little enough for the tribe to feed itself, particularly in lean years. Although they were usually part of larger confederacies, the tribes often made their own alliances and enemies. For many, especially the nomadic clans, raiding their neighbours was a customary and legitimate way of life. Not surprisingly, the caravans would be fair game, and the line between hostile tribes and bandits was often blurred or simply did not exist.

Escorts were therefore a vital part of a caravan, and the emperor's envoys were always accompanied by a large contingent of soldiers, while merchants also hired guards and mercenaries. Every traveller was armed in some way, and they sought safety in numbers, banding together with others to form large caravans with a shared escort. Nevertheless, the threat of being plundered was ever-present—which is one reason why, once links to seaports were established, ships took over large amounts of the caravan trade (although they too faced significant dangers from piracy). Another attraction for using ships, incidentally, was that merchants avoided paying the multiple taxes imposed by rulers, all the way down to even petty chieftains, as goods were transported from one region through to another.

Caravan numbers could swell into hundreds of travellers with thousands of pack animals. The make-up of people was varied as well: other than the merchants and their escort, there were animal handlers, servants, and slaves. Frequently, the caravan would also include private individuals such as monks, migrants, artists, and artisans.

If the caravan was an official one, the envoy or ambassador would prepare a report for his ruler on his return home. Such accounts, as submitted to the Chinese emperors together with those from their military commanders, were later used to prepare the history of the Western Regions and would be included in the *Shiji*. Another important historical source was the records of monks and missionaries, who usually travelled unarmed despite the dangers they faced. Unlike merchants, who guarded any 'commercially sensitive' information they picked up, from religious travellers came a wealth of information about the old Silk Road. More so because they typically traversed large sections of the road, often across many kingdoms. These holy men were educated and, as their writings prove, also very observant. One famous example was Faxian (or Fa Hsien). Accompanied by fellow Chinese monks, he walked through Central Asia to India in search of the sacred books relating to their historical Buddha (meaning 'Enlightened One'). Starting out in AD 399, he eventually returned by sea fourteen years later, before setting down these experiences in his travelogue *Foguoji* (*A Record of Buddhistic Kingdoms*). As well as providing first-hand description of the perils of long-distance travel at the time, his popular account seems to have greatly influenced Chinese perception of India as one similar to themselves: a civilized and culturally advanced society.

The mainstay of the caravan was a pack animal ideally suited for long-distance travel in waterless regions, the highly valued camel.* The local two-humped Bactrian is a supreme example of an animal adapting to harsh conditions. To protect itself from the frequent sandstorms encountered in the desert, it has evolved long eyelashes and nostrils which seal up; and it can sense an imminent storm before it hits, giving the caravan time to prepare. This warning can be vital

---

*   Even in recent times, one camel in Central Asia was roughly worth ten horses or fifty sheep.

as archaeologist Albert von Le Coq discovered first-hand in the early 1900s in the Taklamakan:

> Quite suddenly the sky grows dark . . . a moment after the storm bursts with appalling violence upon the caravan. Enormous masses of sand, mixed with pebbles, are forcibly lifted up, whirled round, and dashed down on man and beast . . . The whole happening is like hell let loose . . . man and horse must lie down and endure the rage of the hurricane, which often lasts for hours . . .

Camels also have an uncanny ability to find water when all seems lost. They can survive long periods without food or water by using their humps to store fat, which is then drawn on for nourishment. The long, shaggy coat the Bactrian grows in winter helps ward off the bitter cold, before being shed quickly with warming weather. The webbing between its two big toes spreads widely as it walks on sand to support its bulky frame while carrying enormous loads. Even when fully loaded, it can gait along at an unbroken pace, marching almost fifty kilometres a day—a feat virtually unsurpassed by other pack animals. But they are known to protest when taken advantage of, as the nineteenth-century Central Asian traveller Arminius Vambery described:

> When the march is too long or the sand too deep, they are accustomed to express their discomfort and weariness. This is especially when they are being laden, if too heavy bales are piled upon their backs. Bending under the burden, they turn their heads round towards their master; in their eyes gleam tears, and their groans, so deep, so piteous, seem to say, 'Man, have compassion upon us!'

To its credit, as a beast of burden, the camel was probably the only animal capable of transporting the necessary loads between the oases of the old Silk Road (wheeled carriages were rarely used then, given the difficult terrain and absence of suitable roads).

Other than camels, there were horses, which some merchants and the more well-to-do travellers rode, while others employed mules or donkeys and many simply walked. As far as possible, they followed geographical landmarks and well-worn tracks which the caravan leader would guide his charges along. Critical to the success of the venture, he would be familiar with the region they crossed, and could navigate by the stars at night if necessary. The route he chose depended on many factors including the weather, trading conditions, and from reports ahead of banditry, civil strife or an outbreak of disease—always, he needed to be flexible. The time of day or night when the caravan marched was largely determined by the seasons. When travelling during daylight hours, caravanners usually got away before first light, stopping to break their fast by mid-morning and eating their main meal late in the afternoon when a halt was called for the day. If called upon, the leader would enforce a brutal yet pragmatic law: *A caravan stops for no one*. Those unable to keep up were left by the wayside, with little chance of survival if an oasis or settlement was not close at hand.

Averaging around six kilometres per hour over most terrain, a caravan could cover between twenty-five and thirty kilometres in a day, which meant that a round trip could take many months or even years, depending on the final destination and travel conditions. However, merchants rarely traversed the length of the Silk Road. Instead, they would work within their own regions, buying, selling, or bartering wares with the next set of traders at bazaars and caravanserais in towns or at frontier posts. At every stage, a profit margin was extracted by the seller and taxes had to be paid to local authorities, thus continually increasing the price of merchandise as it changed hands and moved along the network. Later, as trade developed, transit centres were established at important crossroads, often controlled by the state, where goods could be stocked in large warehouses until the opportune moment presented itself to buy or sell.

The emperor's caravans did, of course, make the round trip, taking several years in the process. Wu Di is known to have had a great love for foreign items and curios. His envoys brought back pearls and gemstones, objects made from tortoiseshell and rhinoceros horn, ostrich eggs from Parthia, and much more. He stocked a park with elephants, peacocks, lions and other exotic animals—including his Heavenly Horses.

Due to the large distance between markets, as opposed to what a caravan could comfortably cover in a day *and* the ever-present threat from bandits, caravanserais began springing up along the routes. For the people of the desert oases, many possessing little arable land and few other commercial opportunities, the caravans were a boon that would transform their small communities. Conversely, an entire settlement was sometimes abandoned if the caravan trade were diverted for any reason. For a fee, the caravanserais would provide much-needed food, fodder, and shelter for travellers, who could gossip and share stories sitting by their campfires at day's end. At these halting places, goods could be traded, animals replaced, supplies purchased, and vital information exchanged about the road ahead. The garrison town at Dunhuang was one such place, as was the city of Kashgar; and on the other side of the mountains, so was the Stone Tower.

Despite the precautions taken by caravans, these were always risky ventures: politically for the envoys, financially for the merchants and, above all, for the physical safety of the caravanners and their animals. With time, empires and kingdoms would decline, but the demand for exotic goods never diminished. Nor did the desire for profits, which were simply too lucrative for the caravans to stop for any sustained period along the Silk Road.

6

The Silk Road

The birth of the Silk Road led to what modern scholars term a *big history* moment—a key event in the development of humanity, as people began concentrating in densely populated cities. It was enabled by what they further describe as 'goldilocks conditions' creating an ideal state of affairs across this network at a point in time, starting with the emergence of stable regimes along its length. These states were wealthy enough to produce surplus goods, which they traded for more than the simple necessities of life. The result was remarkable: a virtual explosion in technological and cultural change as the great empires of the day looked beyond their horizons. Although the Silk Road would ultimately be shaped by the tide of history, during its early years three 'constants' in particular worked as catalysts: the desire for political power, profit, and the exotic.

It would be wrong, however, to portray this 'road' as simply involving east–west exchanges. Even during the First Silk Roads Era, there was trade occurring north–south and in other directions, wherever and however merchants found a way to profit. Similarly, although many modern maps depict 'the old Silk Road', maps that span centuries are by their very nature inexact. They cannot hope to capture changing routes and the multiple kingdoms that existed then, some fleetingly, and many whose names are long forgotten. It was indeed a complex network, which only became more so with time and continued well after silk was no longer a principal item of trade. Although trade may have been the driver, ultimately it was the sharing of *knowledge* that has left a lasting legacy.

Initially, this was a time when Chinese and Greco-Roman ideas poured into Central Asia, which was well placed by virtue of being located in the middle of this exchange. Later, following the decline of the Western Roman Empire (after AD 476), the flow of science and technology was largely from Asia into Europe for nearly 1,000 years—until the *Renaissance* (meaning 'rebirth'), when Europe began emerging from the Dark Ages. Historian Valerie Hansen, begins the conclusion to her book *The Silk Road: A New History* by pointing out:

> [It] was one of the least travelled routes in human history and possibly not worth studying—if tonnage carried, traffic, or the number of travellers at any time were the sole measures of a given route's significance. Yet the Silk Road changed history, largely because the people who managed to traverse part or all of the Silk Road planted their cultures like seeds of exotic species carried to distant lands.

The first part of the journey back east had not been difficult. Their caravan halted to rest and feed the horses and pack animals by the sacred mountain, at a large settlement named Osh where there was brisk trading. Just as he was about to take his leave and return home, another caravan from across the border limped in and spoke of the treacherous conditions they had encountered while crossing the mountains. Their grim news cast a shadow over the caravanserai, and everyone felt the anguish of the people and animals they had been forced to leave behind. With the vague promise of a horse as bonus payment, he was talked into accompanying his caravan over the mountains as far as the Tarim. Which was fortunate as the storm had struck again suddenly and viciously, this time just before the main pass, and had raged most of the day. The horses started to stampede, and many more would have surely died without another handler there to calm them. Thankfully, all the prize horses destined for the emperor's stable survived. Afterwards, the Chinese spoke well of his efforts, and promised to employ him again. When they let him have his pick from the regular herd, he chose a young stallion; one he could never otherwise afford, and whose bloodline he would breed back home. But before returning, he had visited his people once more and ridden for miles across the steppe. Now that he knew the way of caravans, there would be others to join in the future.

After Zhang Qian's return, Emperor Wu and others who followed him began sending out imperial caravans from China. Within decades, their contact with the peoples of Central Asia, particularly the two middle empires, would form a trading bridge all the way to Rome. As middlemen, the Kushans and Parthians levied taxes on caravans passing through their territories in return for protection, even as their merchants bought from the same caravans and on-sold the goods for a profit. The rest of the Indian subcontinent also participated in this trade, but mainly through its seaports. Using the Spice Route, ships rounded the Horn of Africa and sailed along the Red Sea to and from Egypt (the Persian Gulf was also used but carefully controlled by the Parthians).

The prolific export of Chinese goods would help fuel the golden age of the Han Dynasty. From the Roman end, after Emperor Augustus came to power in 27 BC, he initiated a period of stability known as *Pax Romana*, which generated a sharp increase in the demand for luxury items such as silk and spices. The enormous riches from this bourgeoning trade found its way to nobles and merchants alike. An example of this wealth was displayed in the 1930s, when archaeologists uncovered a treasure trove in two storerooms of a Kushan palace near Bagram in central Afghanistan. Amongst the wide array of goods discovered were Indian carved ivory, Roman bronze sculptures, Han lacquer boxes, and Egyptian glass vessels. They were intended for shipment along the Silk Road; and although bales of Chinese silk were not present, this was only because any fabric had probably perished sometime during the 2,000-odd years it had lain buried.

Although distances by sea were greater between east and west, the Spice Route offered a viable alternative for the movement of goods, particularly during times when the Silk Road became too dangerous. Even so, caravans remained key to China for exporting its silk, as lines from a Tang Dynasty poem recall:

> Countless camel bells ring
> Over desolate sands.
> Caravans are travelling
> To Anxi city with silk rolls.

When the rolls finally made it to Rome, the demand for silk there was, by all accounts, insatiable, outstripping supply and driving prices sky-high. Going the other way, however, a trade imbalance existed as fewer goods were as sought after in China. Probably heavier or breakable goods from the west were exchanged at bazaars along the way for items such as furs and perfumes, which were highly valued in the east. But even more than these, there were two 'magical' items which the Chinese most desired: superior horses and dazzling glassware (even coloured glass beads were treated as gems). As goods travelled in both directions, they were subject to taxes at towns and border posts. And to prevent smuggling, the activity of traders was tightly controlled; China, for example, issued passports to caravans stating their destination, the route to be taken, and describing the merchandise they carried.

Rome and Parthia were long-time rivals in this regard, with the former attempting to bypass the latter and break its trade monopoly across the Persian Plateau to avoid paying the high taxes levied by them. The Romans may have controlled the maritime routes arriving from India, but the Parthians would not let them deal directly with the Chinese using overland routes.

Earlier, the two rivals had clashed east of the Euphrates River in the Battle of Carrhae in 53 BC, when mounted archers employing their legendary 'Parthian shot' wreaked havoc on the close-formed Roman legions. Before the day was out, the Romans were routed and suffered one of the worst defeats in their history with 20,000 soldiers dead and half as many again captured, while their opponents suffered only minimal losses. Just before the end came, the Parthians unfurled their brilliantly coloured silk banners. This was reportedly the first time Romans laid eyes on a material that would soon drive their ladies to distraction, even as their state began a love-hate relationship with the Silk Road trade.

The demand for exotic goods in Rome soon reached staggering heights, if Pliny the Elder (AD 23–79) and his famous work *Natural History* is to be taken literally:

> And by the lowest reckoning India, China and the Arabian peninsula take from our empire 100 million sesterces [Roman coin] every year—that is the sum which our luxuries and our women cost us; for what fraction of these imports, I ask you, now goes to the gods or to the powers of the lower world?

Since exports were well below these levels, the trade deficit was acutely felt in Rome. On the other hand, the high custom duties imposed on such items helped pay for the deployment of the Roman legions, on whose victories the state was so dependent. Of this enormous drain of wealth, Pliny notes that at least half went to India in any given year. Amongst its many luxury imports from the subcontinent came prized pearls; incense and perfumes were the speciality of Arabia and raw silk made its way from China.

Initially silk cloth was so rare even the wealthy could only afford small patches which were sewn onto their clothing like jewelled brooches. It was only after more material began arriving via the sea routes, complementing the caravan trade, that silk garments were widely worn by the well-to-do. Even then, it was horrendously expensive. By the third century, it was priced equivalent to Roman gold by weight, worth ten times more than the finest quality linen and forty times the best wool. (A practical reason contributing to its high value was that, unlike cotton or wool, a silk garment does not become a haven for body lice—that intolerable plague found in clothing which was particularly prevalent in earlier times.)

One of the first popular Silk Road historians, Luce Boulnois, who authored two books on the subject, posed the question: 'For what reason was one prepared . . . to pay fabulous prices for a fabric which, until then, one had lived perfectly well without . . .?' Her response applies as much today as it did back then: 'For no other reason than that luxury is luxury and that fashion is fashion.' And the revealing dresses of modern-day celebrities are not so radical as we might think, as the words of the Roman philosopher Seneca suggest:

> I see, too, silken clothing—if clothing that can be called, which does not protect, nor even conceal the body—apparelled in which, a woman cannot very truly swear that she is not naked. Such tissues are brought to us at enormous cost, from nations so remote that not even their names can reach us; and by the help of this vast expense, our matrons are able to exhibit, to their lovers and in their couches, nothing at which the whole public has not equally gazed.

Yet his exasperation was a clear demonstration of the independence and economic power wielded by their women, at least those considered part of nobility. The Roman senate went as far as forbidding their men 'disgracing themselves with the effeminate delicacy of silk apparel', but the ban would not stick. More so because Chinese silk lent itself well to dyeing,* particularly with a colour that would soon come to symbolize religion and power: purple. The dye involved in this colour transformation had to be extracted from thousands of Murex sea snails, making it scarce and expensive. Its production

---

* Although cotton is equally easy to dye, it was not cultivated until much later.

in Phoenician cities, particularly Tyre, remained a closely guarded secret. Pliny also recorded: 'The best Asiatic purple is at Tyre . . . The official rods and axes of Rome clear it a path . . . it distinguishes the senate from the knighthood; it is called in to secure the favour of the gods.' Emperors, generals and the high clergy wore purple silk cloaks, while lesser dignitaries were allowed to edge their togas with it—but women were forbidden the colour unless one was a princess.

As for the silk garments arriving from China, these were often unravelled and rewoven to produce a thinner product that was more transparent and suited to Roman taste. Their poet Lucan, in his epic work *Pharsalia* writes: '[Cleopatra's] white breasts were revealed by the fabric of Sidon, which, close-woven by the shuttle of the Seres, the Egyptian needle-worker pulls out, and loosens the thread by stretching the stuff.'

Despite this fascination with silk and its incredible feel and sheen (early Indians called it 'woven wind'), its origins remained a mystery to Romans, but this only served to enhance its appeal to the masses. The Greek geographer and historian Strabo (c. 64 BC–AD 24) thought it grew in India, while the naturalist Pliny wrote of it as a pale floss growing on leaves. There was good reason for this ignorance on their part, as sericulture was perhaps the greatest industrial secret of all time, jealously guarded by the Chinese for more than 2,000 years. On pain of death, no person was permitted to remove its eggs or cocoons; foreigners were not allowed near nurseries, and guards searched merchants leaving the Jade Gate.

Produced by the domesticated silkworm which feeds exclusively on mulberry leaves as it progresses through its life cycle towards becoming a caterpillar, it winds saliva thread around itself for protection. During this process of turning into a cocoon, it can produce a strand of fine silk up to 1,500 metres long; but it takes approximately 5,000 such cocoons and 200 kilograms of leaves to eventually produce a kilogram of silk.

The technique of unwinding a continuous thread from an intact cocoon was perfected by the Chinese by not permitting the chrysalis to transform into a moth. In fact, after centuries of breeding for this purpose, its wings have shrunk to a point where it can no longer support itself were it to attempt to fly. Nor does the adult moth have a mouth to eat with since it only lives a few days, just long enough to mate and lay eggs. Only the silk of the northern species *Bombyx mori* can be harvested in this way because its thread is stronger and less breakable. This distinguishes cultivated silk from wild varieties, where the moth breaks through the thread to free itself, destroying the thread's continuity in the process. Such wild silks had been available in Rome even before material began arriving from China but had to be combed out and spun (like cotton would be), which resulted in an inferior quality of cloth.

In the first instance, silk had been used by the Han as tribute payments to the nomadic steppe tribes. Later, as the dynasty expanded and exported west, silk evolved from being a luxurious material to one having its own intrinsic value. Since not all of China was monetized during this era, bolts of silk were often utilized as currency. Being readily divisible, they were, for example, used to pay soldiers stationed in the Western Regions, who then exchanged them for goods in the bazaar. And being lighter than coins, the bolts were easier for caravans to haul—records unearthed show an officer would receive two bolts worth 900 coins as his monthly pay. Initially large portions of Han tribute to the Xiongnu were paid in silk, while after 51 BC *all* of it was. Silk was also hoarded like gold: in AD 301, China's treasury held four million bolts in store, each measuring approximately seventeen metres and weighing almost two-and-a-half kilograms.

Other than goods such as silk, spices, gemstones and horses, many other items were also traded during the First Silk Roads Era. Mostly they were luxury articles, but not always, and some could fall into either class: slaves were one such item. War has always been an ongoing and defining occurrence across Asia, and in times past, it inevitably led to the generation of a never-ending supply of slaves. They were amongst the most valuable booty, and as a commodity could be readily used or sold—camels, for example, being the most common form of payment for humans in the Western Regions.

Slavery was primarily a labour (for free) institution, and the great projects of the ancient world would not have been possible without the use of countless slaves, many of whom were craftsmen. To the less skilled fell the bulk of hard labour; and they were also put to work as manual labourers in the fields and mines or as domesticated servants. India was a ready source from where they were marched west across the formidable Hindu Kush. Even centuries later, the Moroccan traveller Ibn Battuta, in explaining how one interpretation of the name of this mountain range name meant 'Hindu killer', wrote: 'Many of the slaves brought to us from India perish while crossing the high passes on account of the severe cold and great quantities of snow.'

All manner of enslaved were also employed in China, as part of an ancient prayer found in Dunhuang, to be recited by a Chinese bridegroom at his wedding ceremony, describes:

> Chinese slaves to take charge of treasury and barn,
> Foreign slaves to take care of my cattle and sheep.
> Strong-legged slaves to run by my saddle and stirrup when I ride,
> Powerful slaves to till the fields with might and main,
> Handsome slaves to play the harp and hand the wine;
> Slim-waisted slaves to sing me songs and dance;
> Dwarfs to hold the candle by my dining couch.*

In fact, slavery was widely practised across most, if not all, countries and cultures of the Silk Road. Captured men were also forcibly conscripted as soldiers, women used as concubines (or worse), and their children in whatever way their masters found most profitable. If a child were born into slavery, its fate would depend on its parents' status and the laws of the land. In some places, if the father was a

---

* Translation by Arthur Waley from *Ballads and Stories from Tun-huang*.

freeman then so was his offspring, whereas in others it depended entirely on the mother.

In discussing human traffic along the Eurasian network, Boulnois writes: 'But, as is revealed in historical texts, more people travelled against their will, and it is they who contributed immensely to the transfer of technical knowledge and religious beliefs, as well as the mixing of peoples.' Other than slaves, many were refugees—a group Hansen designates as 'the most important and influential people moving along the Silk Road'. They fled from conflict and persecution (no different to today), carrying little with them but their tenacity and perhaps skills as artists or artisans to new lands where they sought sanctuary. One example of this type of movement explains how the secret of sericulture was finally revealed—in dispelling the legend, Hansen notes: 'In truth, the know-how for raising silkworms and spinning silk left China the same way that papermaking did, carried by people migrating along the Silk Road.'

Of all the products originating from the east, paper, although not as glamorous as silk, was the most important. Historian James Millward even suggests the Silk Road could just as well be called the Paper Route, so significant was its ultimate impact on the transfer of knowledge through the printed word. The process of papermaking was invented in China and greatly enhanced from AD 105. Initially paper had many other uses, including as clothing and footwear, and its full potential would not be realized until centuries later when its manufacture spread to other nations. One famous example, perhaps, comes after the Battle of Talas in AD 751 when Arab forces defeated the Chinese. Captured craftsmen were taken to the Sogdian capital Samarkand where papermaking was then established—whether this story is true or not, the city soon became renowned for producing the finest quality paper.

Another plant product spread along the Silk Road and processed to great effect was grapes. This time, however, the transfer occurred in the other direction, from west to east. Its seeds were first introduced into China from Ferghana by Zhang Qian when he returned from his initial expedition. It was only later however, around AD 640, that the Sogdians taught the Chinese how to convert grapes into wine, which they soon grew to love, as a warrior's poem from that era reflects:

> With wine of grapes the cups of jade would glow at night
> We long to drink but the *pipa* [lute] summons us
> If we lie drunk on the battlefield, don't mock us friend;
> How many soldiers ever come home?*

Two centuries earlier, it was probably the Sogdians again, who instructed them on making glass—until then a luxury good, which the Chinese coveted as avidly as the Romans did silk. An early text *Bei shi* (History of the Northern Dynasties) describes how this came about:

> [They,] while trading in the Chinese capital declared that they knew how to make coloured glasses from stone. They went and fetched the necessary minerals in the mountains and gave a demonstration . . . the glass they made surpassed that imported from the West . . . A hundred people were taught how to manufacture this glass, which was transparent and brilliantly coloured. All who saw it were amazed and thought it must be the work of a divine power.

Once coloured glassware became readily available in China, it was no longer considered as precious and led to prices falling rapidly—another example, like silk and papermaking, of the loss of an industrial secret resulting in economic consequences that were then felt along an intercontinental trading network.

Although the buying and selling of goods represented the lifeblood of the Silk Road, the spread of religions was certainly as

---

* Prior to making wine from grapes, the Chinese drank rice wine. Strumming the pipa was used to rally troops into battle, much like the bugle.

important, shaping the lives of peoples and nations. All the major beliefs were involved at one time or another, including some that are barely remembered today: Zoroastrianism, Mithraism and Manichaeism. Many historians believe it was the spread of Buddhism, though, that has proven to be the Silk Road's greatest legacy. (Surprisingly, Western scholars did not realize it originated from India until the nineteenth century.) Once, it was the most powerful religion on the subcontinent and across Asia east of Persia; today Buddhism is the world's fourth largest, with over half a *billion* ardent followers. Despite its practice virtually dying out in the country where Siddhartha Gautama (563–483 BC) found enlightenment, his teachings were carried across borders by a great movement of people, including monks and merchants, refugees and slaves.

China was one of the first nations to adopt Buddhism widely, and much of this religion's expansion occurred during the First Silk Roads Era. The genesis of its introduction into China is recorded in the *Hou Hanshu*:

> There is a current tradition that Emperor Ming dreamt that he saw a tall golden man the top of whose head was glowing. He questioned his group of advisors and one of them said: 'In the west there is a god called Buddha. His body is sixteen *chi* high [3.7 metres or 12 feet], and is the colour of gold.' That is why the Emperor sent envoys to Tianzhu [Northwest India] to inquire about the Buddha's doctrine, after which paintings and statues [of the Buddha] appeared in the Middle Kingdom.*

The emperor's envoys returned with a picture of the Enlightened One and a copy of a *sutra* (sermon of the Buddha) which, after its translation, became the first such text in Chinese. During Ming's reign (AD 58–75), the first Buddhist temple was established in the

---

* All translations from the *Hou Hanshu* are by John Hill, including words in brackets.

Middle Kingdom. Later Han emperors would build more, together with monasteries, and make sacrifices to Buddha. After the fall of the dynasty, his teachings continued to disperse; in fact, more rapidly, and even became China's state religion for a time. (Later, during the Tang Dynasty, it became *the* most important religion here for a period.)

The First Silk Roads Era would finally come to an end after three of the four controlling powers—the Han, Kushans and Parthians—collapsed within a matter of years, between AD 220 and 225.* China was divided up by three warlords, while the Kushans and Parthians were overrun by Sasanian invaders. Rome, meanwhile, experienced half a century of instability, when up to twenty-six different emperors reigned, and all but two died violently. At the same time disease epidemics rapidly spread by the increasing movement of people along the Silk Road, contributed directly to its demise. The worst ones became pandemics across continents and had a particularly devastating impact on populations at either end of the Eurasian network—during the Antonine Plague, for example, which lasted fifteen years, up to fifteen per cent of Rome's residents may have perished.

Yet the birth of this network also stimulated trade in a dramatic way, and consequently improved living standards for countless millions. From this wider perspective, historian Susan Whitfield reminds us that: 'The Silk Road is part of all our histories. Far from an ocean of emptiness, Central Asia was the centre of the world, the progenitor of many of civilisations most important inventions, and the crux of world economy.'

Furthermore, ancient China was responsible for much science and technology that modern civilization is built on, including its so-called Four Great Inventions: the compass, gunpowder,

---

* A Second Silk Roads Era (c. AD 600–1000) would coincide with China's 'golden age' during its Tang Dynasty, and the network flourished for a third time under the Mongol Empire (1206–1368).

papermaking, and printing. While from India has come unique philosophy, including two of the four largest world religions—Hinduism and Buddhism—which more than one in five people on our planet today subscribe to.

From the outset, Peter Frankopan tries to correct the often prevalent and misleading Eurocentric view of the past in his bestseller *The Silk Roads: A New History of the World* when he writes in the book's preface:

> The rise of Europe sparked a fierce battle for power—and for control of the past . . . History was twisted and manipulated to create an insistent narrative where the rise of the west was not only natural and inevitable, but a continuation of what had gone before.

Today, the Silk Road is seeing a major revival, driven by China's highly publicized Belt and Road Initiative.* In 2013, President Xi Jinping announced the building of a new Silk Road, investing almost one *trillion* dollars and with the expectation of boosting cross-border trade by more than twice that figure. He has subsequently described it as 'the project of the century' as investment into the project continues to grow unabated. According to some staggering estimates, it will affect more than sixty per cent of the world's population and approximately thirty-five per cent of the global economy. Some commentators and particularly non-participating countries are less than supportive of this revival. They view China's intentions with suspicion and see this as a way of dominating international trade, while unduly increasing its influence. Yet so central is this initiative to China, it was incorporated into its Constitution four years after its unveiling; and is due for completion in 2049, to coincide with

---

* 'Belt' signifies the Silk Road Economic Belt (overland road and rail), while 'Road' represents the modern-day Maritime Silk Road (shipping lanes).

the centennial anniversary of the founding of the People's Republic of China.

Returning to *our* timeline and as the first caravans began venturing west, although the Han nobility understood the value of trading, they considered it an undignified activity. They regarded the merchant class as squeezing profit from their fellow men and, in their eyes, were therefore relegated to low social status. This attitude, together with the vast distances and territories involved, would open the way for other peoples to carve out a share from this emerging network. Two in particular—first the Kushans, followed by the Sogdians—would stake their place as middlemen and, in turn, dominate their section of the Silk Road.

PART II
IN THE HEART OF ASIA

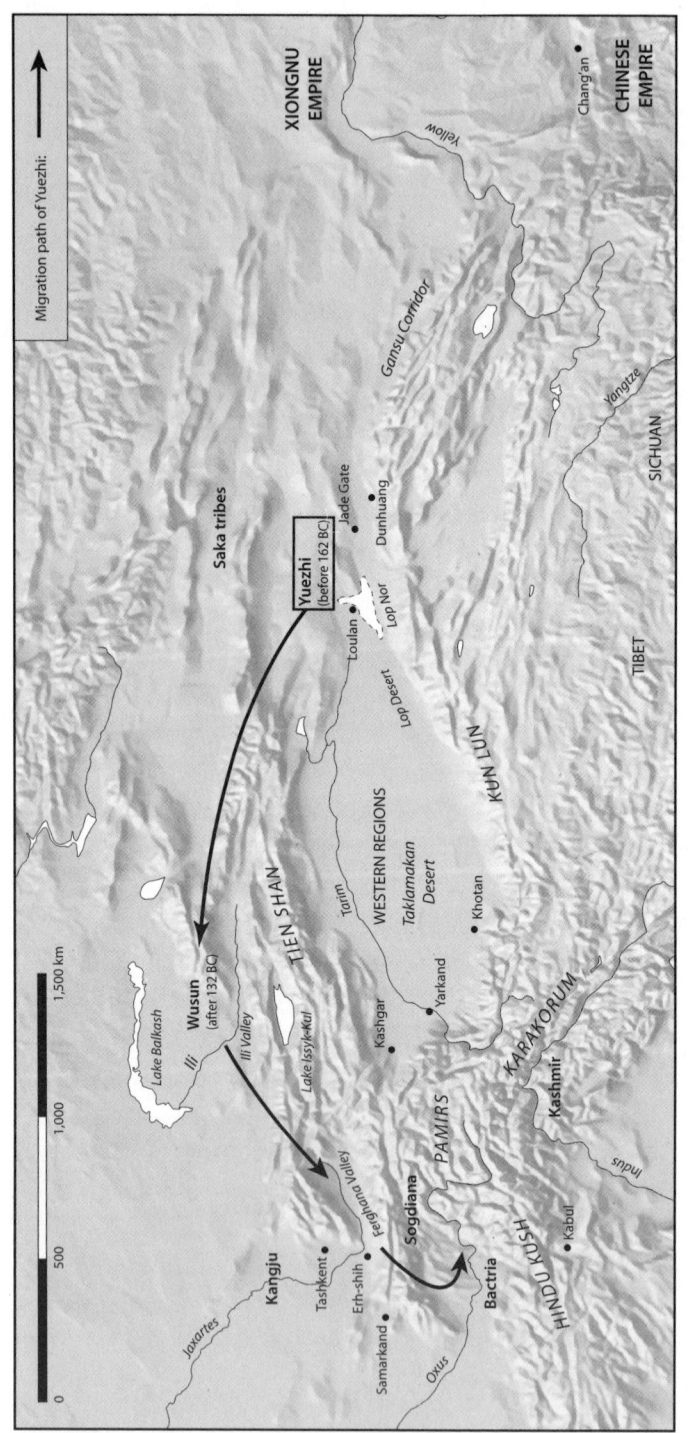

Map 3. Central Asia: marking the migration path of the Yuezhi

7

Migration of the Yuezhi

In 162 BC the Yuezhi nation, together with its herds, began a momentous migration west; one that would start a complex domino effect that would radiate in all directions and, in the process, set the course of history for much of Asia for centuries to come. It would particularly shape the history of India, for the Yuezhi would establish a dynasty that would one day rule large swathes of the subcontinent as the Kushan Empire.

The boy rose early, excited as always to accompany his father to the sprawling bazaar and afterwards to his favourite place, the caravanserai by the river where the incoming camels drank thirstily. Another year and Kang would be twelve—then he could join the caravans and be gone for days at a time, to those new and wondrous places he had heard merchants speak of. Unusually, his family did not live by the bazaar with their fellow Sogdian traders because they needed pasture where Father could breed his beloved horses. He loved them too, especially the fine stallion from Ferghana that had cost a small fortune, but he knew that camels were the key to their success. The elders sometimes whispered how the blood of the steppe showed itself in their family and spoke of Kang's grandfather as a renowned horseman. Father was a good trader too but, although Kang was quick to learn, he could be an impatient teacher. The boy remembered being cuffed hard behind the ear not so long ago, immediately after a desperate seller had left, and gruffly reminded never to show eagerness at the chance of striking a good bargain. He was taught to haggle patiently over every price, and how to recognize the many tricks of the trade—increasing the weight of baled wool with sand being but one. Still, Kang had much to learn; and the bazaar and caravan would be his best teachers.

A few thousand years before the Yuezhi began its migration, these then-pastoral nomads had settled around the Gansu Corridor and Tarim Basin—the *Shiji* locates them somewhere between Dunhuang and the Qilian Mountains. Much of this area was more fertile than it is today, with grasslands watered by streams cascading down from nearby peaks. Here the Yuezhi became more sedentary, establishing agricultural settlements centred about the many oases nestled within this semi-arid region. They were a different people to the steppe-ranging nomads to their north, the Saka tribes which included the Xiongnu. Importantly, the Yuezhi spoke their own language, known today as Tocharian, which further marked them as a nation. Although they left behind no written records, through linguistic variations of their name such as Tuhkara or Tusara, they can be identified from the earliest texts of others, for example, the Indian epics *Mahabharata* and *Ramayana*.* The Yuezhi-Tocharian were known also to Greek scholars such as Strabo and appear repeatedly in Ptolemy's *Geographia*.

In China there were only scant references to the Yuezhi in a few texts until the *Shiji*, when we first learn of them in a substantial way. Sima Qian relates how they began exporting horses and jade to Chinese dynasties prior to the Han. Their only source for jade was the southwestern parts of the Tarim, where it was washed down along rivers flowing north from the Kunlun Mountains. Central to its recovery and trade was the area around Khotan, which lay below the confluence of the Karakash (Black Jade) and Yurungkash (White Jade) rivers, and which continues to yield this gemstone today.

---

*   Both place the Tocharians as living northwest of the modern Indian state of Madhya Pradesh.

A pre-Han economic treatise notes the importance placed on 'the Stone of Heaven' considered to be the imperial gem: 'Our ancestor kings attributed the highest value to jade, as it came from a long distance; gold is second, and copper currency is third.' Jade was considered the link between earth and heaven, bridging life with immortality. Attesting to this, archaeologists have recently excavated a number of burial suits in which some Han emperors and nobility were fully encased, made from hundreds of small jade plates intricately sewn together, sometimes with gold thread.

In the process of exchanging horses and jade for Chinese silk, which were then onsold to neighbouring tribes, the Yuezhi became wealthy. And powerful too, with the ability to field up to 200,000 archer warriors—enough to force the weaker Xiongnu, whom they despised and treated with contempt, to withdraw further north. Proof of their higher status was demonstrated when they received the young Prince Modu as a hostage from the shanyu, as mentioned earlier, but the Yuezhi's superiority would not last.

Their defeat at the hands of the Xiongnu began with Modu's dramatic rise to power, upon killing his father in a hail of arrows. Two years after becoming the new shanyu, he went on the offensive. But despite having 300,000 troops to call on, Modu's first assault was inconclusive, which says a lot about the Yuezhi's strength. Repulsed but not defeated, Modu would spend much of the next thirty years subjugating other steppe tribes to the north instead, as well as raiding south into Chinese territory. Then, after concluding a peace treaty with the Han, the Xiongnu turned their attention back to their old enemy, this time with devastating consequences. In a letter to the Han emperor in 177 BC, Modu boasted of his army commander's success: 'Through the aid of Heaven, the excellence of his fighting men, and the strength of his horses, he has succeeded in wiping out the Yuezhi, slaughtering or forcing to submission every member of the tribe.'

The Han court, knowing the might of the Yuezhi, was suitably impressed by Modu's report of victory. Its high officials counselled the emperor to continue their fragile peace with the Xiongnu rather than risk losing a war against them. In fact, Modu's claim was an exaggeration, and it was his son and successor Jizhu, fourteen years later, who led the Xiongnu to decisively defeat the Yuezhi on their third attempt, before turning the skull of their king into a drinking cup. Incidentally, the Han only learnt of the Yuezhi's defeat more than two decades *after* the event, which explains why Emperor Wu did not seek an alliance with them sooner (through the likes of Zhang Qian).

The Yuezhi, once a proud and powerful nation but now expelled from their homeland, began their long exodus deep into Central Asia. They still retained a force of some 100,000 archer warriors, which gives some indication to the size of their migration, possibly comprising half a million men, women and children. And, of course, many times that number of livestock, representing their remaining wealth. One can imagine the preparation and anticipation in the lead-up to those fateful days—it would have been a sight to behold: The noise and excitement of people and animals milling about as the various tribes finally got underway after loading their wagons. Millions of hooves kicking up dust; sheep and goats herded along by scurrying children; mothers minding their babies, as others took care of the elderly and the pack animals. And all the while, mounted warriors guarded the flanks and rear, even as outriders scanned the horizon for possible further attacks by the now-dreaded Xiongnu.

As it turned out, some of the Yuezhi tribes, for reasons not explained by the Grand Historian, were unable to make the journey west. Instead, this group, known as the Lesser Yuezhi, would relocate a shorter distance and move southwest to the edge of the Tibetan Plateau, seeking refuge amongst the local people there. Initially, the Greater Yuezhi (or Da Yuezhi) had also hoped to move just beyond the reach of their enemy. They headed northwest into the fertile Ili Valley, a trek of some 1,800 kilometres, before settling somewhere by the waters of the idyllic Issyk-Kul (meaning 'warm lake').* Here, the

---

* Issyk-Kul's waters never freeze due to underground volcanic activity; and it is the world's second largest saline lake after the Caspian Sea.

Yuezhi seized the surrounding land after defeating the local tribes, who were an eastern concentration of the Saka confederacy which lay sprawled across the Eurasian Steppe.

Once forced out, these Saka tribes began their own migration south to the Indian subcontinent, adding to the domino effect that would permanently change the make-up of Central Asia. Although the routes they took are somewhat conjectural, it is thought that after splintering into three groups, each began their own substantial journey into India. One group came through the high Pamirs to settle permanently in Kashmir, braving their way through a torturous trail famously referred to as the Suspended Crossing (or Hanging Pass), as described in the *Hanshu*:

> [A] path that is [0.5 metre] wide, but leads forward for a length of thirty *li* [12 kilometres], overlooking a precipice whose depth is unfathomed. Travellers passing on horse or foot hold on to one another and pull each other along with ropes . . . When animals fall . . . they are shattered in pieces, and when men fall, the situation is such that they are unable to rescue one another. The danger of these precipices beggars description.

A second cluster of Saka crossed the Hindu Kush and continued further into the Punjab; while the third group took a circuitous route, approaching from the southwest, before settling in present-day Sindh and expanding around Gujarat.* According to Indologist Sten Konow, the Saka ultimately 'became the great intermediators through whom Indian civilization and Indian ideals spread to Central Asia and the far east'.

Meanwhile, the Greater Yuezhi had hoped to have found their new home after arriving at Lake Issyk-Kul and the Ili Valley. This first leg of their migration can be corroborated through

---

* Here they established the powerful Saka Kingdoms and initiated the Saka Era from AD 78—a milestone in the historical Indian calendar, still used today for traditional and religious purposes.

linguistical analysis using Ptolemy's *Geographia*. Archaeologist Y. A. Zadneprovskij suggests further evidence comes from discoveries of many *podboy* tombs (underground chambers with a side niche) used to bury their dead, and the north–south orientation of the bodies together with some of the artefacts placed in these graves. Although historians are not in agreement regarding the details of these events, whatever pathway the Yuezhi took to arrive at the lake, their almost thirty-year stay in this idyllic region was not to be permanent.

The Wusun, their immediate neighbours when they had previously resided in Gansu, now took revenge for past grievances. A decade before the start of their forced migration in 162 BC, the Yuezhi had attacked the Wusun when they were a smaller state, killing their king, seizing their lands, and forcing them to flee into the arms of the Xiongnu. The *Shiji* relates how the dead king's son, Kunmo:

> . . . then only a baby, was cast out in the wilderness to die. But the birds came and flew over the place where he was, bearing meat in their beaks, and the wolves suckled him, so he was able to survive. When the Shanyu heard of this, he was filled with wonder and, believing Kunmo was a god, he took him in and reared him.

The Wusun prince grew to manhood amongst the Xiongnu and successfully led troops into battle for the shanyu, who then appointed him king of his own people. Once they were strong enough to break free, however, Kunmo led them away and declared the Wusun an independent nation. He steadfastly refused to attend the Xiongnu court, while his warriors were able to repulse their attacks trying to bring the Kunmo back in line, highlighting the might of the Wusun by this stage—the *Hanshu* records their population as being over 600,000 and their fighting strength at almost 200,000 warriors.

Now Kunmo saw an opportunity to avenge his slain father and seek redress for their people. In perhaps what was a surprise attack, in 132 BC his warriors inflicted a crushing defeat on the already displaced Yuezhi. After seizing their lands for themselves, the Wusun settled down permanently in the Ili Valley (where Zhang Qian, on his final expedition, had tried unsuccessfully to convince the Wusun to return east and pressure the Xiongnu).

The dejected Yuezhi had no option but to uproot once again and continue their exodus even deeper into Central Asia.* This time they headed southwest, first passing quickly through the Ferghana Valley, perhaps wintering there and, to their relief, without meeting resistance from the local population who lived in fortified towns. All the while, they left behind their dead in telltale *podboy* tombs, but little else for archaeologists today to reconstruct their flight. Perhaps in the spring of 131 BC, they continued into the state of Kangju and probably along the Zerafshan Valley, which lay in the heart of Sogdiana. Such a large body of armed foreigners would have seemed threatening to these locals as well but, yet again, the Yuezhi seem to have passed through peacefully. Possibly, the Sogdians convinced them that 'more suitable' land might be found further on, beside a great river. Thus in 130 BC, more than three decades after being forced out from their homeland in western China by the Xiongnu and a migration of over 3,500 kilometres, the Yuezhi arrived in northern Bactria on the banks of the mighty Oxus.

Before they could settle down here, however, in the river valleys north of the Oxus, the Yuezhi had to overcome the people already living there. Two centuries earlier, the conquests by Alexander of Macedon—or Alexander the Great, as he is better remembered— had effectively joined the Occident and the Orient. Following in the wake of his armies, Bactria had been turned into a Hellenistic (meaning 'Greek-like') homeland for colonists who introduced their language and script here. Yet this was an age-old land, thought to be the traditional home of Zoroaster's religion and one of the earliest

---

* Some tribes of the Yuezhi, and indeed the Saka before them, chose to remain and be absorbed into the Wusun confederation—a familiar occurrence then, leading to a frequent mixing of ethnicities in Central Asia.

centres of civilization in Asia. Its capital Balkh was already 1,000 years old when it fell to the Greeks; but after the death of Alexander and the carve-up of his vast empire, Bactria became a satrapy of the Seleucid Empire. Its people eventually broke free around 250 BC to form their own Greco-Bactrian Kingdom, conquering Sogdiana in the process and eventually extending their reach into northwestern India, along the Indus Valley and neighbouring parts of the Punjab.

Initially a sedentary society with an economy based around agriculture and well known for its vineyards, Bactria became a sophisticated and thriving kingdom, with its traders ranging across Central Asia. A third-century Roman writer Justinus would colourfully describe it as: 'The famed Bactrian Empire of a thousand cities, wallowing in wealth.'* Its coinage was of the finest quality, even better than in Greece itself, and Strabo's description of the country's prosperity noted:

> And much of it produces everything except oil. The Greeks who caused Bactria to revolt grew so powerful on account of the fertility of the country that they became masters, not only of Ariana [eastern Persia], but also of India . . . and more tribes were subdued by them than by Alexander . . .'

After a century of prosperity, however, Bactria began disintegrating when it was overrun by Saka tribes (a different group to those ejected from the Ili Valley by the Yuezhi). Although the Saka hordes may not have sacked its cities, their presence eventually led to the collapse of the Greco-Bactrian Kingdom around 125 BC. Similarly, renowned historian and numismatist A. K. Narain relates the fate of these Greeks in India:

> It is the story of the rise of an adventurous people to fill the vacuum created by the absence of a great power; when, in

---

* His epitome remains an important source regarding the nomadic migration in Central Asia.

course of time, new peoples came on the scene, one had to give way to the other . . . Their kingdom fell, and their proud ruling families merged with the mingled racial stocks of north-west India, until all traces of them were lost.

In Central Asia, the overthrow of the Greeks was a key moment in history, recorded at the time by Strabo while writing about the Saka: 'But the best known nomads are those who took away Bactria from the Greeks . . .' Furthermore, historian W. Barthold points out that this was 'the first event of world history recorded both in Western (Greek) and Far-Eastern (Chinese) sources'. The latter came from Zhang Qian's account in the *Shiji*, after his first expedition when he finally caught up with the Yuezhi here. Sima Qian recorded the envoy's description of the now crumbling Bactrian kingdom, a shadow of its former self: 'It has no great ruler but only a number of petty chiefs ruling the various cities. The people are poor in the use of arms and afraid of battle, but they are clever at commerce.'

As the domino effect triggered by the displacement of the Yuezhi wound to an end, they would make one last migration before disappearing from history as a people. Fifty years after first settling on the northern fringes of this kingdom, they crossed the Oxus south into Bactria proper towards 80 BC and wrested control from both the Saka and the remnants of the Greeks living there. Within a century, the descendants of the Yuezhi would reappear in history, only this time not as a tribal confederation but as the Kushan Empire.

8

The Kushan Empire

The Kushans were one of two key middlemen during the First Silk Roads Era (the other being the Parthians). Moving goods between Rome and China, they would unify the overland Silk Road between the Oxus and Ganges rivers and establish themselves as cosmopolitan masters of northern India. Much of their prosperity also came from controlling the maritime trade between the Indian and Roman ports and, in doing so, they were able to circumvent the Parthians and their high taxes levied on caravans. In the main, the Kushans kept peace with their neighbours, creating the stable conditions crucial to promoting trade and cultural exchange. Their rule as a family dynasty would last over two centuries; and after their fourth king Kanishka came to power around AD 127, the subsequent so-called Great Kushans era has been described by Narain 'as one of the great periods of world history'.

Yet in comparison to the other three Silk Road empires, frustratingly little is known about them from when the Yuezhi-Kushans first migrated into Bactria, as they did not produce any great historian nor possess a script of their own. Moreover, there is no consensus about their borders or chronology; Benjamin regards the Kushans as 'one of the most important yet least known agrarian civilizations in world history'. Even the span of their rule—for our purposes AD 25 to 225—is one of the most disputed in Asian history. We know of their pathway into Bactria as the once-migratory Yuezhi almost entirely from the *Shiji* and *Hanshu*. But after this, large gaps emerge as to how they established themselves in the northern half of the Indian subcontinent, spilling into Central Asia and even parts of China within the Tarim Basin.

Kang and his father were in the bazaar buying the last of the merchandise for their journey. Always on the lookout for bargains, they carefully sought out small, high-value items: spices, perfumes, precious stones and the like. The caravan from the east was due any day now, led by the Kushans who had already made their trade with the Chinese at the border, accepting bolts of raw silk in exchange for horses and exotic items. Father and son would join the many merchants and hundreds of pack animals with their own heavily laden camels. Kang could manage two now, while his father led a string of four, and the groom he had employed from the steppe would guard their two fine horses with his life. When the caravan arrived, his father would seek out its leader and, after presenting him with a small gift, ask permission to join them. In his case, he was always welcome and often consulted, as he knew this section of the road stretching towards Parthia, particularly where the lesser-known wells were located. In the desert of the black sands, the bones of dead animals were always a grim reminder of the consequences of not finding sufficient water.

Before the birth of the Kushan Empire, the first half of the Han Dynasty (206 BC–AD 9) had already come to an end, together with its chronicles in the *Hanshu*. The history of the dynasty's second half, as recorded by Fan Ye, is continued in the *Hou Hanshu* (Book of the Later Han). Although written some two centuries after the demise of both the Later Han and the Kushans, the author's account is generally regarded as credible by modern scholars. Unfortunately, the record of how the Yuezhi nation became the Kushan Empire is described in only a short section within one of its chapters. Upon crossing the Oxus, for reasons unknown, the Yuezhi split into five tribal divisions, each with its own *yabghu* (prince) and occupied various areas in and around Bactria. Their governing structure was adopted in part from the peoples they displaced and their neighbours, but their administration did not reach all the way down to village level and collect tax from farmers. Instead, Indologist Harry Falk argues that each tribe controlled a portion of the trade route passing between Parthia and China, or down into India and its burgeoning seaports. (Based on this work, Falk went on to suggest a location for Ptolemy's Stone Tower, but more about that later.)

By protecting the caravan routes, the *yabghus* and their tribes profited immensely from this arrangement and grew into international traders themselves, learning to deal with other merchants in many different currencies, languages and scripts. In this way the Yuezhi-Kushans emerged as prime middlemen of the Silk Road, ready to cash in on the great entrepôt of increasing Eurasian trade. No doubt, they learnt a good deal about the art of trading from the wealthy Bactrians whom they had unseated. In their adopted homeland, the Yuezhi-Kushan presence was strong, comprising 100,000 households with a population four times that number. Eventually the five tribal divisions were reunited, as the *Hou Hanshu* records:

> More than a hundred years later, the prince of Guishuang, named Qiujiuque [Kujula Kadphises], attacked and exterminated the four other princes. He established himself as king, and his dynasty was called that of the Guishuang [Kushan] King . . . All the kingdoms call [their king] the Guishuang king, but the Han call them by their original name, Da Yuezhi.

The new Kushan king soon led his armies across the Hindu Kush to conquer Kabul, and then Kashmir. A chapter in the *Hou Hanshu* suggests he also exercised influence over the Western Regions of China around Kashgar, Khotan and other states in the Tarim Basin. This information resides in a chapter titled 'Biography of Ban Chao', an army general whose father and siblings had compiled the earlier *Hanshu*. Ban Chao (or Pan Ch'ao, AD 32–AD 102) was charged with protecting Han interests in the Western Regions and may have permitted the Kushans to exercise limited economic control in the Tarim in return for assistance against their common enemy, the Xiongnu. Either way, from the second century onwards the Kushans extended their influence all the way to the kingdom of Loulan, which also became Indianized until the fourth century, after which the region ran out of water and declined.

Other than dominating northwestern India, the Kushan Empire expanded across the Oxus to include parts of Sogdiana and Kangju in their sphere of influence. The *Hanshu* noted that their 'way of life is identical' and the Kushans would cement their relationship with the people of Kangju through marriage into their ruling family. Historians find the northern boundary of the Kushan Empire vague and difficult to pin down, and whether it incorporated the southern sections of Sogdiana or Kangju is uncertain.

After ruling for around sixty years (c. AD 25–85), Kujula Kadphises died aged eighty-four—a ripe old age for those times. His son Vima Taktu succeeded him and continued to expand their empire. But he seems to have overstepped the mark with Ban Chao when, a few years after taking the throne, he proposed an alliance with China by way of marriage to a Han princess. Although he had first sent through tribute, which included antelope, lions and jewels, the general was apparently affronted by his audacity. Ban Chao denied the Kushan envoys safe passage through the Western Regions to the Han capital, where they had intended presenting their king's proposal to the emperor. This refusal angered Vima Taktu, so much so that two years later he sent a column of cavalry to enforce his wish—70,000 mounted archers, if figures in the *Hou Hanshu* are to be believed.

To enter the Tarim, the horsemen faced an arduous trek through the Pamirs, perhaps using the Suspended Crossing. Once there, however, the Kushans found that the wily Han general would not engage his forces with them. Realizing that this arid and sparsely populated region would not support a force as large as the intruders, Ban Chao instead focussed his efforts on denying them sustenance, cleverly employing a 'scorched earth' tactic. Meanwhile, his troops captured a contingent dispatched by the Kushans to neighbouring states in the hope of bolstering support—after beheading several hundred of them, the Han made a display of their heads. Unable to land a blow in battle and exhausted from lack of provisions, the Kushans had no alternative but to concede. After extracting an apology, Ban Chao let them return home, marking an end to the only recorded armed incursion by the Kushans into China.

For his success in securing the west, Ban Chao was installed Protector General of the Western Regions the following year. Always a bold soldier, ready to seize the initiative in battle, he held the view that 'he who does not enter the tiger's lair will never catch its cubs'. A modern-day statue of him, standing tall in a memorial park in Kashgar, recalls the exploits of one of China's greatest generals and statesmen.

As for Vima Taktu, little is known of him after this incident, although his reign presumably would have been a short one considering the longevity of his father. In fact, the *Hou Hanshu* does not even mention him and marks the incursion into the Tarim as the work of his son, the third Kushan ruler, Vima Kadphises. However, there definitely were two Vimas, who between them ruled for over four decades after the death of Kujula. This much is known after a chance discovery was made in 1993 of a 'document' known as the Rabatak Inscription. Dating back to AD 100–150, it comprises twenty-three lines of Bactrian (Greek) script chiselled onto the face of a rock.

The rock in question is a rectangular limestone slab measuring approximately one metre by half a metre and weighing over half a tonne. It was found on a hill known as Kaffirs' (Unbelievers') Castle in the northern Afghan village of Rabatak by the mujahideen while digging a trench (the site has yet to be properly excavated by archaeologists). An aid worker assisting with landmine clearing subsequently took video footage of the rock and forwarded it to the British Museum, where numismatist Joe Cribb recognized it as similar to another inscription uncovered at a nearby archaeological site. With the help of expert linguist Nicholas Sims-Williams, the Rabatak Inscription was painstakingly deciphered. It reveals, up to that point, a royal lineage of four kings: Kujula, followed by the two Vimas, before Kanishka ascended the throne. A few lines taken from the script describe the incumbent and his rule: 'Kanishka the Kushan, the righteous, the just, the autocrat, the god worthy of worship . . . In the year one there was proclaimed to India . . . and he submitted all India to (his) will.'

As to the illustrious rock itself, it was feared lost after going missing during the Afghan Civil War. Thankfully, it was located a few years later after a low-level government clerk suggested a search in a local depot of the Department for Mines, where it was indeed found. Slightly damaged but with the script still intact, it resides today in the National Museum of Afghanistan.

Unfortunately, the fragmentary documents and inscriptions discovered to date only go a little way towards piecing together Kushan history. Critical evidence comes from another source altogether, numismatics; and the many thousands of coins unearthed over the years bear testimony to their story. In fact, the legend on these coins represents the only other extant writing generated by the Kushans, thus making their study critical.

Unlike most objects made from naturally occurring materials—such as wood, fabrics and leather—coins made from metal are obviously less likely to perish with time. Being mass produced, they also have a significantly higher rate of survival and therefore discovery. Even today, old coinage from as far away as Rome can be found in the bazaars of Asia, sometimes after being picked up by farmers while tilling their fields. Importantly, the *script* on these coins, although somewhat limited, provides hard evidence of the reign of past dynasties and their rulers. And since each monarch would typically issue new coinage upon assuming power, most can be readily dated.

Where these coins are found is also of importance. Areas across northern India and Central Asia in which Kushan coinage has been discovered help mark out the extent of the empire and the reach of their trading activity. Conversely, for example, the extreme rarity of finds in Sogdiana proper suggests that their northern neighbours had probably maintained their independence. Whereas a study by Cribb of Kushan coins found in Khotan provides further evidence of their direct economic and political control of this important Silk Road city.

The *style* of their coinage tells its own story. During the Yuezhi-Kushans migration into Central Asia and India, they encountered the Greeks and Romans whose influence is clearly visible on Kushan coins. For example, their strongman Hercules is depicted on the reverse side of some issues; while Kujula's early portraits were clearly inspired by their emperors, reflecting the contact between Rome and India. His mint was largely based on Greek practices and copied styles from the regions he conquered. Although initially starting out with the simple *yabghu* title on his coinage, on achieving greater victories he began bestowing on himself grand titles such as *Maharaja Rajarajasa Devaputra* (Great King of Kings, Son of a Divine Being).

Kujula's grandson Vima Kadphises began issuing the first gold coins of India, re-minting vast amounts of Roman currency making its way into Asia. His coins are also distinctive for portraying his large frame, huge nose, and a wart on one cheek. During the first half of the Kushan dynasty, the weight of its gold coinage was kept remarkably consistent, thereby adding to the stability of their trade. The Kushans would adopt Bactrian as their official script (using the Greek alphabet) and as one of their official languages, which they called Aryan. In fact, during this period, Bactrian was one of the world's most important languages;* and by inscribing their coinage with Greek letters, the Kushans ensured their currency was widely usable across the Silk Road. (Greek tradition would also have a profound and lasting effect on Kushan culture in many other ways.)

These coins also tell a story about religious beliefs. Similar to the Greeks and Romans, Vima Kadphises started attributing divinity to his royal personage by associating with the gods through currency. His son Kanishka would go even further, being the first king in recorded history to show a halo above his head on his coinage, leaving

---

* Bactrian remained in use for over six hundred years after the Kushan Empire, thus enduring for a thousand years as a language of culture.

no doubt of his supposedly divine status. He is typically shown making a sacrifice over a fire altar—signifying that Zoroastrianism, which originated from Persia, was the central faith during the Great Kushans era. There are also depictions of Greek and Indian deities on Kushan coinage, both Hindu and Buddhist, suggesting a tolerant and encompassing view of other religions.

In fact, one of the earliest surviving images of the historical Buddha can be found on Kushan gold coins, of which only a handful have ever been discovered. Interestingly, he is depicted standing with his feet pointing outward—as steppe men would, from spending considerable time on horseback; while the accompanying Greek letters BODDO make it clear as to who the image represents. On the obverse side, the king stands in a similar posture dressed in steppe-style robes and trousers, while his inscription declares *Raonanorao Kanirki Korno* (King of Kings, Kanishka, of Kushana).

Figure 4. Kushan coinage: coin on top shows Kanishka (obverse) and Buddha (reverse); coin below shows another king with artificial skull deformation (obverse)

A controversial coin which perhaps unlocks more history is a double-busted piece that has generated considerable speculation. It has the face of Vima Kadphises on one side and, most unusually, a *second* king's portrait on the reverse. In the latter's case, no name is ever given on any of his own coins which are found in abundance, only titles such as *Soter Megas* (Great Saviour), leading to him being labelled the Nameless King. Since the Rabatak Inscription named only four kings, some numismatists understandably conclude that Soter Megas was the same person as Vima Taktu. But Narain is convinced 'he has to be placed earlier than Kujula and that . . . he is no other than the Nameless founder of the Yuezhi state of Bactria'. Others think he may have been a temporary ruler, even a usurper of sorts; or possibly a local governor from the Indian part of the empire who replaced the short-lived Vima Taktu—not being a true descendant of the royal house, he may have refrained from identifying himself on coins. Whichever view proves correct, as more coins are found and classified, further Yuezhi-Kushan history continues to be revealed.

Another insight into Kushan royalty evident from their coinage is the practice of artificial skull deformation—the binding of a child's head to produce a desirable conical shape—the result of which can be seen on some of their statues as well. (Unfortunately, the sculptures of many, including the famous life-size statue of Kanishka, are missing their heads—deliberately knocked off, but when and for what reason remains unknown.)

Kanishka expanded his nation's territory to probably its greatest extent, heralding the start of the empire's high point. His reign of some twenty-six years, beginning around AD 127, witnessed many caravans criss-crossing the Silk Road, and during this time Ptolemy would complete his *Geographia* (although he did not mention the Kushan Empire by name). When Kanishka took the throne he declared the start of a new era, which he signified by engraving his coins from 'Year 1'. This designation had initially caused historians some confusion as it seemed to imply that he was the founder of the Kushan Empire, but the Rabatak Inscription clarified this. His milestone year may have also marked the Kushan invasion and conquest of the Ganges Valley—the *Hou Hanshu* briefly mentions an 'Eastern Division' of the empire as quite separate and distant from its Bactrian heartland. The text also describes an independent Tianzhu (Northwest India) and its people:

> Their way of life is similar to that of the Yuezhi [Kushans], but the country is low, humid and hot. This kingdom is beside a great river [the Indus]. The people ride elephants into battle. They are weaker than the Yuezhi [Kushans]. They practice the Buddhist way, not to kill, or wage war, which has become the custom.

Like the Mauryan emperor Ashoka the Great four centuries before him, Kanishka is also remembered as a great patron of Buddhism, leading to its proliferation throughout Asia. The same routes first taken into India by the nomadic tribes, the Saka and Yuezhi, served as pathways out for monks—hence, this route is sometimes referred to as the Buddhist Road. Using this trail to cross the Pamirs and settle in the Tarim Basin, Indian migrants also spread the word, together with the deeds and depictions of the various *bodhisattvas* ('enlightened beings' who delayed attaining Buddhahood to help others first).

Just as Ashoka initially standardized the Buddhist doctrine, Kanishka is venerated for convening a similar council, this time in Kashmir, which led to the emergence of a second branch of Buddhism known as *Mahayana* (Great Vehicle). Recalling the work of this second council, Xuanzang would comment: 'The great meaning of the scriptures has once more become clear, and the subtle worlds have again been elucidated.' The travelling monk described how Kanishka had the scriptures engraved on copper plates and deposited in a specially built tall *stupa* (Buddhist monument housing relics) some 500 years earlier, but unfortunately these plates have never been found. Xuanzang witnessed the edifice they had been housed in, as had one of his predecessors, the equally famous Faxian, who described it as: 'more than forty chang [122 metres] high and adorned with all precious metals. Of all the stupas and temples ever seen . . . there was none that could be compared with this one for beauty and majesty.'

Monks such as Faxian and Xuanzang, other than unwittingly becoming some of history's greatest explorers and travel writers, also became key translators. When Buddhism began its spread into the Tarim and beyond, its scriptures were initially captured in Chinese through a two-step process. A teacher, usually from India, recited and explained a memorized Sanskrit text to his local students, who then transcribed it. This often led to a corruption of the translation because their understanding of the scriptures and any technical terms was inadequate, while the teacher, unable to read Chinese, could not check what his students had written. An example was the term *bodhi* (meaning 'enlightenment') which was erroneously recorded as *tao* (meaning 'the way'). In their quest to acquire and faithfully reproduce Buddha's teachings, Faxian, Xuanzang and other monks worked out a system to transcribe foreign languages, for example Sanskrit into Chinese—which then absorbed some 35,000 Sanskrit words and terms that it retains today. And the efforts of the monks themselves have not been forgotten, as Boulnois notes: 'In Chinese Buddhism, more than in any other religion, the translators have been remembered and honoured.'

In Sanskrit literature, the Enlightened One is referred to as the *Mahasarthavaha* (Great Caravan Leader) for leading his followers to *nirvana* after having eliminated human suffering. A disciple of his, the Indo-Greek king Menander, in describing his lord to a converted Bactrian king, explained that Buddha 'is like a caravan leader to men in that he brings them beyond the sandy desert of rebirths'. Kushan merchants were particularly attracted to his teachings and, perhaps surprisingly, its strong commercial philosophy, as historian Xinru Liu points out by quoting the advice offered in *Dialogues of the Buddha*:

Whoso is virtuous and intelligent,
Shines like fire that blazes [on the hill].
To him amassing wealth, like roving bee
Its honey gathering [and hurting naught],
Riches mount up as an ant-heap growing high.
When the good layman wealth has so amassed
Able is he to benefit his clan.
In portions four let him divide that wealth.
So binds he to himself life's friendly things.

One portion let him spend and taste the fruit.
His business to conduct let him take two.
And portion four let him reserve and hoard;
So there'll be wherewithal in times of need.*

Such advice was consistent with Kushans positioning themselves as middlemen on the Silk Road, enabling them and their caravans to thrive; as Liu again notes: 'For merchants, making donations was a much more satisfying and practical approach than self-denial.' Together with many of the rich and powerful, they reciprocated by becoming great patrons of the religion, channelling some of their wealth into its monasteries and temples, adorning them with great artworks, silk and gems to make them seem like paradise. They also created images of the Buddha and had his sutras copied out in an effort to acquire the 'merit' needed to escape the cycle of suffering and rebirth. As religious demand grew for the 'seven gems' of Buddhism (such as gold, silver, crystal, lapis lazuli, carnelian, coral and pearls) it promoted further exchange between India, China and Central Asia in these high-value, low-volume items which were ideally suited for the caravan trade.

In terms of Kushan culture and its recording, as well as Bactrian, they adopted an ancient Indian script—Kharosthi—to write down their various dialects. For a while, from their base near Gandhara

---

* Translated by Thomas and Caroline Rhys Davids.

(northern Pakistan and eastern Afghanistan), their tongue even became the *lingua franca* of the Tarim, and documents written in Gandhari using the Kharosthi alphabetic script have been recovered in oases there. Some knowledge of their culture has also survived through their art forms, as the Kushans were notable for their patronage of art schools. It was in their famed workshops in Gandhara and Mathura (northern India), connected by the Indian Great Road (later to become the Grand Trunk Road), that the Buddha image was first conceived. Previously, he was only alluded to with symbols such as footprints or an umbrella, but *never* in physical form. This radical departure is considered by many art historians as the Kushans' greatest contribution to the art of Asia, and its spread into China gave rise to what is today termed Serindian art.* Together with the distinctive Greco-Buddhist paintings and sculptures of Buddhist holy men, all wearing pleated togas, they represent superb examples of the cultural syncretism thriving on the Silk Road. The artists of Gandhara had probably never heard of Greece nor appreciated the full extent of the 'road', yet their famed art schools were funded by the wealth generated from this trade network.

Kanishka is regarded as the greatest of the Kushan kings. He would be followed by two others before the dynasty began its steady decline, sometime after AD 225—a story again reflected in their coinage, which begins to show deterioration and debasement. During most of the First Silk Roads Era, the Kushans were the great merchants of Central Asia, playing such a critical role that Benjamin suggests his designation of this period could also be labelled the Kushan Era. After their decline as middlemen, they would be replaced by another people: traders who had started out as their apprentices but whose time had now come—the Sogdians.

---

*   Serindia was a term coined to describe Chinese Turkestan, which lay on the route between Seres and India.

9

Sogdian Traders

Sogdiana occupied a special place along the Silk Road and the geography of Central Asia—on both counts, lying at its heart. The Xiongnu roamed the steppe to its north; the Kushan Empire sat on its southern border; China lay to the east; while the Parthians occupied their west and Rome being still further west. Even before the First Silk Roads Era, the Sogdians already had an illustrious history, and a rich future lay in store. Not only would their capital Samarkand be regarded as the most splendid city in the world one day, theirs would also be the greatest caravanner network across Asia. But although their 1,600-year time span would significantly outlast the Kushans, they too would ultimately disappear from history as a people.

The caravan began arriving late in the afternoon, straggling in now that there was no threat from bandits this close to town. The pack animals, although heavily loaded with Chinese goods, were in fine shape. The onward journey to Parthia was only starting, and the march from the mountains along the Ferghana Valley was an easy one. Kang was quickly amongst them, greeting the older traders he knew with respect while bantering with their boys—his lively personality made him a favourite. He could speak several languages, some better than others, mostly picked up in the bazaar. There was also time to learn during the long marches and in the evenings by the campfires; but only after his never-ending chores were done, as care for the animals came before all else. Learning many languages was essential for any would-be trader, although his native tongue was gaining in usage along this stretch of the road. More so as their written script became commonly used, and the Sogdians placed a high value on teaching their sons to read and write from a young age. Kang was known for his ability, often being called out by illiterate traders to read a simple contract or write a note, sometimes even on paper. There was one chore he did not mind, and that was having to collect the incoming mailbag and scamper through town delivering letters.

Sogdiana was centred around the Zerafshan River and its marshy lower reaches—in earlier times and during wetter years, the river actually flowed all the way into the Oxus. Its people inhabited the many fertile valleys and waterways including the Oxus and Jaxartes, the twin rivers which formed its natural frontiers and marked out a region also referred to as Transoxiana. Outside these rough borders lay Kangju to the north and the Ferghana Valley to the east (where Zhang Qian had first encountered the Sogdians). They were an Aryan people; the first written reference of their country marks them as a satrapy of the Achaemenid Persian Empire (550–330 BC) together with Bactria. The Sogdian language, although their own, was derived from their powerful Persian neighbour, as were their writing and religious practices, which followed the teachings of Zoroaster.

More is known of early Sogdian history than of the Kushans who 'mentored' them, but written records are still scant and mainly from external texts such as the *Shiji* and *Geographia*. The *Mahabharata* also mentions the Sogdians, when it describes them allied with the Kauravas as they make ready to fight an epic battle with their cousins, the Pandavas: 'And the Tusara [Yuezhi], the Yavana [Greeks] and the Saka, along with the Culika [Sogdians], stood in the right wing.'*

Before they became predominantly traders, the Sogdians had lived in small independent city states and fought battles of their own. Of particular note was their resistance to the conqueror who most

---

* Translation by P. C. Roy as quoted by Vaissière in *Sogdian Traders*.

left his mark on Central Asia, Alexander the Great. His invading army of 329 BC would Hellenize these lands, eventually leading to the establishment of the famed Greco-Bactrian Kingdom eight decades later. Before that, after subjugating the region, this twenty-seven-year-old conqueror went north to campaign and found yet another city, this one to be named Alexandria Eschate*. It was being built on the Jaxartes, to guard against intrusions from the Saka 'barbarians' of the steppe. At this point, true to their character, the Sogdians revolted, as historian Ulrich Wilcken explains:

> [The] Bactrians and Sogdians had a very highly developed, proud national feeling, and a tenacious enthusiasm for freedom and independence, such as Alexander had found nowhere in the Persian Empire, with the exception of Tyre and a few other brave mountain tribes . . . They would hear nothing of submission to this foreign Macedonian . . .

Under their leader Spitamenes and supported by neighbouring Saka tribes, the Sogdians besieged a Greek garrison in Samarkand (then known as Maracanda). When Alexander sent a relief army south, it was annihilated by the Sogdians, who inflicted the worst defeat of his career. In the months that followed, however, his generals regained lost territory and extracted revenge, putting an estimated 120,000 to sword. Spitamenes escaped to the steppe and fought on, employing hit-and-run tactics. But he was eventually betrayed by his weary Saka allies, who sent his head to Alexander, suing for peace. This event effectively spelt the end of the Sogdians' military might, and their independence.

Other than the sheer extent of his conquests, Alexander stands out for his readiness to integrate culturally into the lands he conquered. He encouraged his men to intermarry with local women and adopt their customs. In Bactria-Sogdiana, he would controversially marry one of their high-born, the captured Princess Roxana, after having

---

* Literally 'Alexandria the Furthest', by present-day Khujand.

been reportedly smitten by her beauty. Following Alexander's untimely death, their unborn son, who would be named after his father, was in line to inherit the throne upon coming of age but was executed with his mother before he could do so.

Another Sogdian notable was Apama, daughter of Spitamenes. Alexander would arrange for her marriage to one of his generals, Seleucus, who would eventually succeed him in Asia and found his own dynasty. Upon his death, their half-Sogdian son Antiochus would rule the Seleucid Empire, which ultimately would last for two-and-a-half centuries; at its height stretching from the Mediterranean Sea to the Indus River.

On Sogdiana's border lay the Greco-Bactrian Kingdom, of which it had been a part before the Saka invasion around 130 BC. Even prior to these events, individual Sogdian city states had never united to form a dynasty in their own right; and from this point onwards their political history vanishes for several centuries.

Their commercial story, however, makes its first appearance now in eastern records, through a historically significant reference in the *Shiji* as detailed below (remembering that Sogdiana lay *between* Ferghana and Parthia). Other than pointing out their origins, Sima Qian described them as keen traders:

> Although the states from Da Yuan [Ferghana] west to An-hsi [Parthia] speak rather different languages, their customs are generally similar and their languages mutually intelligible. The men all have deep-set eyes and profuse beards and whiskers. They are skilful at commerce and will haggle over a fraction of a cent.

More importantly, historian and author of *Sogdian Traders* Étienne de La Vaissière points out:

> The stakes are clear: if Da Yuan is Ferghana, the skilful merchants living to the west of Da Yuan, between it and

Parthia, can only be the Sogdians, and we would then have the founding text for the history of Sogdian commerce.

Interestingly, Sima Qian's description also came to underlie the iconic Sogdian male image: deep-set eyes above a hooked nose and bearded face, looking out from under a peaked hat while engaged in trade. But the Sogdians were more than just traders, in possession of a rich history and culture; and after supplanting the Kushans, their own tongue became the *lingua franca* of the Silk Road.

Sogdiana is not named specifically in the *Shiji* because, during the period when these records were compiled (around 100 BC), it was no longer a nation with diplomatic status and thought to be answerable to Kangju. Following Zhang Qian's initial visit, Emperor Wu's envoys had travelled beyond the Western Regions with their caravans. Unfortunately, many of these Han officials were not as trustworthy as the man who had shown them the way, as Sima Qian again notes:

> When the envoys returned from a mission, it invariably happened that they had plundered or stolen goods on their way ... The envoys were all sons of poor families who handled the government gifts and goods that were entrusted to them as though they were private property and looked for opportunities to buy goods at a cheap price in the foreign countries and make a profit on their return to China.

The Sogdians would have participated vigorously in this caravan trade, and the 'leakage' of goods and profit that resulted from it. Initially they operated at the lower levels, by targeting the envoys' supply personnel and menials. It is probably the influx of Han caravans that kick-started the Sogdians into large-scale trading. In the formative years, they were 'the low wage earners' as Vaissière describes:

> In the shadows and on the margins, the Sogdians may then have taken the full measure of the importance of their geographical

position as the last urbanized territory before the world of the steppe and, by virtue of this fact, an obligatory route for some of the Chinese embassies and the precious products they carried.

Other than receiving caravans, the *Hanshu* records Sogdians as taking the initiative to travel east 12,300 *li* (5,000 kilometres) in an attempt to trade in the Chinese capital. This text contains a section titled 'The state of Kangju' (which included Sogdiana); and quotes from a report by the Protector General of the Western Regions, who complains:

> Kangju is behaving arrogantly, even refusing to treat our envoys with the respect that is their due . . . The king and noblemen take their food and drink first, and when they have finished they then have the officials of the protectorate general served with theirs . . . If in view of these considerations we ask why [Kangju] sends its sons to attend [at the Han court], [we find] that desiring to trade, they use a pretence couched in fine verbiage.

From such reports, Vaissière concludes that 'the beginnings of long-range Sogdian commerce can thus be firmly dated to a few decades before our era [BC], following a century of commercial contact between Chinese envoys and petty Sogdian traders'. In stark contrast, four centuries later they would become the *dominant* foreign merchants in the Gansu Corridor, and for several centuries afterwards remain the primary traders who led long-distance caravans across Central Asia. Amongst the many items traded, they would transport alfalfa to the Chinese for the horses they had obtained from Ferghana. And going west, they would supply silk to the Persians (although they were not permitted to trade beyond their common border). This expansive reach would set the Sogdians apart, as most other merchants did not participate in distant itineraries, preferring instead to deal within their own regions.

During the first centuries AD, the principal trade route from China, in fact, passed *south* of Sogdiana through the knot of high mountains, before shifting down the Indus Valley to reach the ports of India. At the time, this trade and territory was controlled by the Kushan Empire. Nevertheless, the independent Sogdians were enthusiastic participants, with merchants and monks moving readily between centres. As 'students' of the Kushans, Sogdian traders even emigrated to their flourishing cities in search of commercial gain; Vaissière points out: 'The situation in Sogdiana at the time was very mediocre in comparison with the brilliant urban civilization of the Kushan Empire.' Evidence of their movement and activity can still be seen today from graffiti carved by Sogdians on rocks in the upper Indus Valley, attesting to their early presence in India. Many hundreds of such examples were discovered at remote sites following the completion in 1979 of the Karakoram Highway, the famous high road linking Pakistan and China. A decade later, Sims-Williams, one of only a handful of researchers in the world able to read Sogdian, translated the longest of these inscriptions:

(I), Nanai-vandak the (son) of Narisaf have come (here) on (the) ten(th day) and asked a boon from the spirit of the sacred place K'rt that . . . I may arrive at Tashkurgan more quickly and see (my) brother in good (health) with joy.

Another example of movement by merchants comes from a Chinese statesman in 25 BC, as recorded in the *Hanshu*. He discusses the visit of Indians from Kashmir to the Han capital after negotiating the Suspended Crossing but goes on to complain that 'there are no members of the royal family or noblemen among those who bring gifts; the latter are all merchants and men of low origins'.

Monks, too, travelled between the centres. Together with the Sogdians, they were the principal propagators of Buddhism into China. An important sixth-century text, *Gaoseng Zhuan* (Biographies of Eminent Monks), lists hundreds of Buddhist holy men active there. One biography, dated around AD 250, explains the motivation of an orphan to join a monastery and, in doing so, he makes mention of Sogdian merchant families living in Tianzhu (India):

> The ancestors of the Sogdian Seng hui were people originally from Kangju who had lived in Tianzhu for several generations. His father went to Jiaozhi in order to trade there. When [Seng hui] was about ten years old, both his father and mother died. After having grieved with great filial piety, he left the world.*

Other than contacts with India, proof of Sogdian trading networks stretching all the way into China would come from a remarkable chance find of a mailbag containing eight letters somehow lost in transit. These so-called Ancient Letters would shed light on Sogdian history like no other documents to date. Together with the graffiti found on rocks, they represent the oldest body of surviving text written in the earliest form of the Sogdian language and script. The story of their discovery in 1907 and the journey of the discoverer— including his efforts to find the Stone Tower—offer a fascinating tale of archaeology and exploration.

---

* Translation by Édouard Chavannes as quoted by Vaissière in *Sogdian Traders*. Note: Jiaozhi lies in present-day northern Vietnam.

10

The Archaeological Explorer

Aurel Stein was born in Budapest in 1862 and grew up in the then-powerful Austro-Hungarian Empire. His first name was, in fact, Marc, but he rarely chose to use it. The third child of middle-class Jewish parents, he and his older brother were baptized as Protestants for reasons explained a century later by his biographer Jeannette Mirsky: 'Stein's parents . . . knew [then] as did all Jews in Central Europe, that their religion barred them from participating in Western culture. Jews were not only legally confined to ghettos . . . they were not permitted in schools, universities, and professions . . .'

At home Stein grew up speaking Hungarian and German, before learning Greek, Latin, French and English at school. At university he studied Sanskrit and Persian—yet, despite his impressive linguistic skills, his inability to read Chinese would come to haunt him later, during his finest scholarly moment.

With any luck his father would have sold their goods before they reached Parthia; that way they would not have to pay taxes at the border. Then they could turn for home early—the nights were already cold, even in the caravanserais. Besides, a quick turnaround meant more journeys and higher profits in the long run. But he knew Father would not part with either horse except for the asking price. Perhaps he might find a buyer as they passed through Bactria, as the descendants of the old Greeks knew a good horse when they saw one, and their coinage was readily accepted everywhere. Before returning home, they might go north first to see his grandfather's people, who always welcomed them. His father was still drawn to the steppe but visited less and less these days. It would depend on where they could buy merchandise for their return trip. Certainly, they would not go north with loaded camels as it was off the main caravan trails, making it too risky to travel on their own. There were fewer caravanserais out that way, but they would have no trouble finding shelter for the night in one of the many yurts that dotted the steppe. When the day came for Kang to lead his own caravan, as he knew it would, his knowledge of this endless grassland and its people would surely be invaluable.

As a young boy, Stein was given a copy of *The Campaigns of Alexander*, written in the second century AD by the Greek chronicler Arrian, which he read avidly. Throughout his life, it would inspire him to retrace the marches undertaken by the Macedonian army, including identifying what he believed was the lost site of Aornos, where they had spectacularly conquered a mountain fortress in northern India. Similarly, he followed the ancient journeys of other great travellers through the heart of Asia, and keenly sought out Ptolemy's landmark on the old Silk Road.

Stein completed his doctorate in Indology and Old Persian at a German university while he was still twenty, before receiving a government grant to pursue postdoctoral studies in England where he learnt yet another language, Punjabi. His unfailing efforts in learning native tongues would serve him well throughout his career, as he once wrote: 'The true door to a knowledge of its people leads through their language.' Stein was, however, prepared to interrupt his studies and return to Budapest to complete military service. During this obligatory year-long exercise he learnt surveying and map-making—skills that he would put to good use later as an explorer. On returning to England, he picked up another handy skill, numismatics, by studying old coin collections held in museums there. Although formal training was not available in archaeology then, he read voraciously on the subject and learnt from the work undertaken by others. Always smartly dressed, with a stocky and military-like appearance, Stein's short stature belied his physical strength and endurance.

Without the means or contacts to secure an appointment at a major European university, Stein decided to sail for the subcontinent in 1887 to take up a dual role: Principal of the Oriental College in Lahore and Registrar of Punjab University. Little did he know that India would effectively become his home, and one he would grow immensely fond of. Before long he discovered Mohand Marg, a high alpine meadow in Kashmir where he would retreat during the summer months, and which became his spiritual home. In this idyllic spot he would set up his tent to read, research, and write up his many expedition reports long into the night by lamplight. Although a 'loner' almost by necessity, Stein was a great letter writer too, maintaining lengthy correspondence with family, friends and scholars in Europe throughout his years—letters which would later provide valuable insight into his life's work and motives.

Stein's first success came as a direct result of the early years spent in this mountainous state. With dogged determination, he tracked down the *codex archetypus* (the original copy of all extant versions) of a rare twelfth-century manuscript, *Rajatarangini* (Chronicle of the Kings of Kashmir). Written in Sanskrit verse by Kalhana, a local pandit and India's earliest historian, it records the history of the kingdom and its rulers as related in eight books going back several millennia, and is therefore of vital interest to Indologists. Although the work—a mix of legend and reality—suffers from chronological errors, particularly its early books, Kalhana's account does contain genuine elements of history; for example, he records the Kushan Empire, Kanishka and his compatriot kings.

Stein quickly realized that it was impossible to fully examine this chronicle without first understanding the region's topography from an historical perspective. This prompted him to research and publish *A Memoir of the Ancient Geography of Kashmir*. Then, with grateful and critical assistance from local pandit scholars, over the course of a decade, Stein completed his English translation of *Rajatarangini*. It was published in 1900 with copious notes in two volumes to lasting acclaim. Interestingly, in a footnote, he revealed how the borrowed *codex archetypus* was almost lost after being accidentally dropped in the harbour during his voyage to England. It was, as he sheepishly noted, 'recovered only with difficulty', but fortunately 'the soaking with sea water left no perceptible trace in the codex'. Stein closed his preface to *Rajatarangini* stating: 'I have spared no effort to serve this end, and in the result of my labours, I hope, there will be found some return to the boons I owe Kashmir.' A decade later, he would hand over his valuable collection of Sanskrit manuscripts, comprising over 350 items, to the Indian Institute Library—a legacy to his beloved Kashmiris and their rich history.

The turn of the century saw Stein start out from Mohand Marg to explore and excavate in Chinese Turkestan (once known as the Western Regions, today Xinjiang province). This would be the first of three major Central Asian expeditions spanning 1900–01, 1906–08, and 1913–16.* The eminent archaeologist Leonard Woolley described these expeditions as 'the most daring and adventurous raid upon the ancient world that any archaeologist has attempted'. Stein's efforts, together with a small number of other explorers such as his equally famous contemporary Sven Hedin, would initiate a field of work known today as Silk Road Studies—its first phase encompassing the period from the 1890s to the early 1930s.

---

* A fourth expedition in 1930–31 was cut short after Chinese authorities forbade further excavations.

Figure 5. Aurel Stein (inset) and his caravan in the Taklamakan Desert

Stein's travelling parties were never large; almost always he was the sole European, employing only a handful of trusted men, while relying on local labour to do the clearing work at the various excavation sites. He always took a specialist surveyor along, loaned from the Survey of India, the institution which would later prepare maps from the topographical data they gathered. For his second and third expeditions, he hired a Chinese secretary and language teacher Jiang Siye (or Chiang Ssu-yeh), who proved to be a faithful and cheerful friend as well. Years later, Stein had good reason to describe him as 'the best scholar who ever helped me in Asia'. There was one other much-loved member who tagged along: Stein was forever accompanied by a dog. Over the years as one dog died or he had to leave it behind in either England or India, he replaced it with another—always a fox terrier, bar once. All would be named Dash and referred to in Stein's writing as Dash I–VII.

The hallmark of Stein's expeditions was meticulous military-style planning and execution, critical for success when literally venturing 'off the beaten track' as he invariably did, sometimes not laying eyes on another European for over a year. He would need to go deep into the Taklamakan Desert to seek out potential sites, often taking many days to get there. (The oases of the Tarim Basin could not, themselves, yield a great deal in the way of archaeology—having been irrigated for centuries, the fields were covered by thick silt, rotting any old wood and most items of value buried underneath.) While exploring, Stein made good use of Hedin's recently published work *Through Asia*, a two-volume account detailing his travels and the difficulties encountered in this region.

Before he could start out from India, Stein spent a great deal of time and effort securing backing and funds from the government; although his constant requests seeking leave from work to devote increasingly more time to exploration would often exasperate his employer. His persistence in getting his own way with other bureaucracy also raised many an eyebrow—the secretary of the Royal Geographic Society once commented: 'As usual I found that despite my best efforts I had been defeated by Stein.' When the need arose, Stein made good use of the contacts he had carefully cultivated, including appealing directly to the Viceroy of India for support even if it meant bypassing his immediate superiors and ruffling their feathers. But his doggedness was mostly driven by sheer necessity, for example, when obtaining travel passports from the Chinese, without which he simply could not proceed.

To meet his caravan's never-ending expenses, Stein carted around various local currencies including rupees, roubles, and copper coins, as well as silver horseshoes—the latter being cut into smaller pieces before being carefully weighed out. Of greater concern for the caravan was the physical challenge of getting into the Tarim Basin; including finding a way through the mountain barrier along perilous tracks and negotiating the high passes between northern India and Xinjiang. The return trip was just as hazardous, often laden with bulky archaeological finds, well boxed-up but still requiring careful handling. Sometimes the items uncovered were too delicate to remove, in which case, as Stein noted, he would 'bury them again safely in the sand after they had been photographed and described, and trust that they would rest undisturbed under their protecting cover'.

Due to the extreme heat and lack of water in the Taklamakan during the warmer months, Stein had little alternative but to excavate during winter and put up with the cold. (Hedin's foray into the desert during *spring* had nearly cost him his life.) Stein would later describe the cold nights:

> When the temperature had gone down in the tent to about 6 degrees Fahr. below freezing-point [-21°C], reading or writing became impossible, and I had to retire among the heavy blankets and rugs of my bed . . . Still it was uncomfortable to wake up with one's moustache hard frozen with the respiration that had passed over it. Ultimately I had to adopt the device of pulling the end of my fur-coat over my head and breathing through its sleeve!

At least the freezing temperatures enabled his caravan to transport blocks of ice, loaded on many specially hired camels and donkeys, to be melted later to provide potable water. When they could, wells were dug, but the water from these was often brackish and insufficient for both men and animals. Hauling adequate food and fodder into the desert was another challenge, although here the hardy Bactrian camels came into their own, being able to survive on only a quarter litre of rapeseed oil daily. At times the desert terrain was so hard on the camels' feet, that it cut their soles to the point that the handlers would sew oxhide onto their footpads. But Stein's feet would suffer a worse fate during one expedition when, after experiencing severe frostbite, he had three toes amputated—to prevent the onset of gangrene and possible loss of his legs.

On his first expedition, Stein took his party north through Kashmir along what is today the Karakoram Highway—of course, no such road existed then, just rough tracks. To haul their gear, depending on the ground conditions encountered, Stein used ponies, yaks, or dozens of hardy hillmen as porters. On ascending the Roof of the World, his caravan passed east of Afghanistan's Wakhan Corridor and the source of the Oxus, where three imperial powers then converged: the British, Russian and Chinese empires.

Soon after crossing the Chinese frontier into Xinjiang, they arrived at Tashkurgan (or Taxkorgan), once capital of the ancient kingdom of Sarikol, with its massive stone fort sitting on a hilltop. There was something else historically important about this town, as Stein would later point out in his expedition report *Sand-Buried Ruins of Khotan*:

> As far as local observations go, everything tends to support the view first expressed by Sir Henry Rawlinson, that Tashkurgan, [meaning] 'the Stone Tower', retains the position as well as the name . . . which Ptolemy . . . knew . . . as the emporium on the extreme western frontier of Seres.

Other than Ptolemy's *Geographia*, during his expeditions Stein referred to various early texts in an attempt to identify places and routes described by famous travellers—Alexander the Great, Marco Polo, and Xuanzang were amongst the notables whose footsteps he followed keenly.* In terms of locating the Stone Tower, however, Stein would change his mind after a later expedition, deciding that Ptolemy's midpoint on the Silk Road was not at Tashkurgan after all, but that it lay elsewhere.

He learnt of the legend surrounding Tashkurgan's stone fort by consulting Xuanzang's writings, after the monk had stopped here on his travels. It had been built for a Han princess whose journey, while being escorted by an envoy to marry a Parthian king, had been interrupted due to local warfare. For her protection, the envoy placed her on a solitary peak, accessible only by ladder and under

---

* In terms of the first, Stein detailed this quest in his book, *On Alexander's Track to the Indus*.

constant guard for three months until the fighting ended. However, it was then discovered that she was with child, and a local attested to seeing a spirit from the sun, mounted on horseback, visit her every day. Seeing this as a disgraceful situation, rather than resuming their journey west, the envoy built her a palace on a rocky peak in Tashkurgan. Here, she gave birth to an extraordinary boy who grew to become king. Xuanzang recorded that on his death, this king's remains were placed in a nearby cave which, by virtue of not decaying over time, proved his divine birth.

During his first expedition, Stein concentrated on excavating ruins in the vicinity of Khotan, making good use of Xuanzang's *Records of the Western Regions* to help identify holy places and settlements claimed by the desert sand—the latter he labelled 'terminal oases'. Always meticulous, he would carefully survey an area and its sites before digging, then keep detailed records of all items unearthed, no matter how small or seemingly insignificant. But to his dismay, Stein found that local treasure seekers had previously scoured many of the sites, spurred on by demand from European collectors for antiquarian items. They would burrow into partially buried dwellings or stupas looking for anything of value but were limited to foraging at shallow depths and hunting for easy pickings. Under Stein's direction, his hired labourers dug deeper, removing tonnes of material over many days to uncover Buddhist shrines and monasteries. They revealed antique sculptures and painted murals with a distinctly Indian influence; while hundreds of old coins, fragments of silk and carpets, and small terracotta figurines were found at multiple sites. The Gandhara sculptures unearthed, once created in Kushan workshops, allowed Stein to trace the diffusion of an ideology about which he would write: '[The] spread of Buddhist religion and literature over Central Asia and into the Far East is the greatest achievement by which India has influenced the history of Asia in the past.'

Hundreds of documents were recovered by Stein written on paper, leather and wood in various scripts. So numerous were these Khotanese documents that their processing by experts in Europe and the publication of a complete catalogue would take a century. Some of the writing reveals the trials of everyday people—one poignant example being the practice of *milk payment*: When dire circumstances forced parents to put their children up for adoption, they would join their new family either as a free member or a slave. If payment, usually a horse, was not forthcoming, the child was used as a slave.

Amongst the finds, to Stein's astonishment, here in faraway Chinese Turkestan on yet-unopened documents were clay seals impressed with images of Greco-Roman gods, including the likes of Hercules. A selection of these, together with others opened later to reveal their contents, can be viewed today in New Delhi; the exhibit's sign begins with the statement: 'These documents on small wooden tablets are amongst the most valuable possessions of the National Museum.'

One of Stein's most striking discoveries was a simple wooden panel painted in black and white with a curious picture. It shows an attendant with outstretched arm pointing to the hairpiece of her noble lady, as a four-armed deity looks on while holding weaving implements in his hands, and another lady sits at a loom.

Figure 6. Wooden panel depicting how the secret of sericulture was lost

Again, Xuanzang's writing would provide an explanation: The legendary scene described how the secret of sericulture, so jealously guarded in the heartland of China, was finally lost to the Western Regions (sometime after AD 440). Apparently, a Chinese princess was due to marry the king of Khotan and live there permanently.

He warned his wife-to-be that if she wished to continue wearing silk, she would have to bring the means of its production with her as no such material was produced in his kingdom. Horrified at the thought of not being able to wear silk, the princess smuggled the eggs of silkworms and seeds from the mulberry tree in her elaborate hairpiece. (Approximately 1,500 eggs weigh one gram and have a ten-month incubation period, which would have made such transportation possible.) Relying on the guards at the Jade Gate not to search her hair, the subterfuge worked and gave birth to a flourishing silk industry in Khotan which has endured to this day.*

Before he returned with his finds to Kashmir, Stein attended to one other task that had been troubling him, and one which remains the bane of all historians and archaeologists—a clever forger. This particular deception centred on a batch of manuscripts which had come to light a few years earlier in the Tarim. Written on paper in an ancient Indian script but in a language unknown, it had greatly excited academics in Europe, especially the professor deciphering them. He also happened to be Stein's close friend and patron, who had earlier pronounced them to be genuine. However, when hundreds of similar manuscripts and crudely printed books continued to be offered for sale, based on the genuine articles he had unearthed, Stein smelt a rat. He knew the ground conditions where these books were supposedly unearthed were such that they were unlikely to have survived; and, furthermore, no block-printed texts had ever been found in this area. Stein confirmed his suspicions after examining one of these manuscripts in Khotan and subjecting it to his 'water-test'—the ink writing readily dissolved when dabbed with a wetted finger.

He tracked down the treasure seeker who was offering these items and interrogated him closely over two days. To begin with, the Khotanese man vigorously protested his innocence, but when it

---

* A century later, two Nestorian monks similarly smuggled eggs out in the hollows of their staffs, to reveal the secret of sericulture to Europe.

became obvious that Stein had caught him lying, he confessed fully. Although his early forgeries were based on genuine fragments, upon realizing that his European buyers could not read the script anyway, each of his men began inventing their own 'ancient characters'. They were penned on dyed paper and 'aged' over a fireplace, before being sprinkled with sand to simulate their supposed excavation. The master forger went on to explain how, when they could not meet the demand for handwritten material, he and his cohorts turned to block-printing to increase their output. Knowing the harshness of the local justice system, Stein chose not to report the forger. But, by understanding his production method and bringing back one of the printing blocks, he could now show scholars how to identify these fakes and save researchers in Europe countless months needlessly trying to decipher them.

As for Stein's own finds from around Khotan, they would keep specialists busy for *decades*, deciphering and cataloguing his historical treasure trove.

11

The Hidden Library

Kang was tired but happy as they were almost home now. The trading had been good throughout, and there was a lot to see while delivering the contents of his mailbag. His father had haggled long and hard over his prize horses with the many buyers they had attracted, before parting with both for a small bagful of gold staters. Exactly how much Kang was not told, but enough that he had bought him a scroll in the same bazaar. Scribed on parchment, it told the story of his heroes who had fought Iskander's Greek army. Afterwards, the caravan had a stroke of good luck in finding the Oxus frozen over, saving them the cost of being ferried across at Amul. But the nights were bitterly cold, especially when they headed into the desert of the black sands, away from the caravanserais. Water had been hard to locate at first; they had struggled on to the main wells where they were permitted to draw its brackish water by the local tribe, but only after parting with a bag of silver. The camels had proved their worth once again when many of the other animals fell, exhausted. Just as they finally made it out of the desert, a dozen stragglers had been ambushed—by the time some of the guards from their escort rushed back, the brigands had fled leaving behind only stripped bodies to bury. Kang's father had managed to sell the rest of their goods in Merv, again after hours of haggling. Then they joined another caravan coming back east, and past Bukhara they had broken off and headed for the steppe.

It was during his second expedition starting in 1906, by gaining access to what is sometimes referred to as the Hidden Library, that Aurel Stein would achieve lasting fame—but infamy in some sections as well. Before this life-changing event, however, other major discoveries awaited him.

Stein entered the Tarim Basin and made his way along the shores of the 'wandering' Lop Nor lying within the Lop Desert. During the late glacial period, the whole basin was one vast salt lake; of which the Lop Nor is the last disappearing survivor, having largely dried up today.* Its position has seemingly wandered over time due to the shifting desert and changing flow of the Tarim River, which carries fresh meltwater and empties into it.

By referring to Hedin's map, Stein was able to locate the old ruins of Loulan, yet another oasis settlement swallowed up by the shifting sands. Here, amongst other finds as he described later, he discovered 'fragments of a woollen pile carpet, the earliest so far known, and a small bale of yellowish silk, fairly well preserved'. The latter would prove significant because: 'this bale shows us the regular width, nineteen inches [48 centimetres], and the actual form in which that ancient and most famous product of Chinese industry used to be carried to the classical West.' Other evidence of this city being on the old Silk Road came from items such as glass beads, bronze arrowheads and, during a later expedition, two hundred Han-era copper coins which he picked up along the lake bed. The coins were square-holed and 'seemed as if fresh from a mint'. Lying in a straight line on the salt-encrusted clay, they had obviously come loose from the string which bound them, before gradually emptying out of their bag as a caravan or an army column trudged along. This was the route taken by Marco Polo six hundred years earlier, when he described his crossing of what he called the 'Desert of Lop' (which included the Taklamakan).

Just north of Dunhuang (meaning 'blazing beacon'), Stein ran into what he would term the Chinese *Limes*: a series of defensive

---

* In 1941, it was measured as being 80 km long and 40 km wide. More recently, the area around Lop has been used by China as its nuclear test site.

watchtowers, walls and forts representing the western extremity of the Great Wall started by the Han.* Although it had suffered from decay in places, the wall was over two metres thick and stretched 600 kilometres. He tracked it for much of the way, often by sighting one watchtower from the previous one. They were solidly built from sun-dried clay bricks and for centuries would have been manned by soldiers. The lookouts could report any threat down the line within three days using smoke signals by day and flaming torches at night. Many towers stood over five metres high and were connected by low ramparts with a sandbank on the outer side. The presence of intruders during the night would have been detected by keeping the sandbank swept clear and regularly inspecting it for telltale footprints, although this seems to have been an unpopular duty with the patrols.

Around the towers and adjoining soldiers' quarters, from vile smelling 'rubbish heaps' (many containing age-old human excrement), Stein and his men retrieved hundreds of records. Some proved to be imperial edicts, while other discoveries of military orders included correspondence with the Protector General of the Western Regions. They were mostly written on long strips of wood, which Jiang Siye was able to decipher and date to the first century AD. Stein later wrote: 'It thus became certain that this ruined border line was occupied already in the Former Han dynasty's times, and that I had in my hands the oldest written Chinese documents so far recovered.' Some were scribed on strips of silk—proof of its use as a writing material before the invention of paper—and gave 'exact details as to the place of production, size and weight of the bales from which they had been cut off'. Writing to a friend, Stein spoke of the freshness of his finds and a sense of *déjà vu*:

> I feel at times as I ride along the wall to examine new towers, etc., as if I were going to inspect posts still held by the living . . . Two thousand years seem so brief a span when the sweepings

---

* Similar to Roman *Limes* (plural: *limites*), which was built to mark out and defend the Roman Empire's limits.

from soldiers' huts still lie practically on the surface in the front of doors or when I see the huge stacks of reed bundles as used for repairing the wall still in situ near the posts . . . I feel strangely at home here along this desolate frontier—as if I had known it in a previous birth.

Despite the age of these watchtowers, many were remarkably well preserved because of the lack of wind erosion. Stein, to his amazement, witnessed this stillness first-hand after returning here seven years later, on his third expedition 'to recognise my own footprints and in some cases even those of my ever-active fox terrier Dash II'.

In the twelfth tower, badly decayed though it was, his men picked up a major find, although no one at the time realized its real significance. Later, Stein described how the Ancient Letters were found:

> [From] a refuse-filled room at one of the watch-posts on this section we recovered not less than eight neatly folded letters written on paper in the Early Sogdian language and script of which before my second expedition nothing was known. A few were found wrapped up in silk covers while others were merely fastened with string . . . [The writers] must obviously have preferred the newly invented writing material, paper, to the wooden slips and tablets to which Chinese conservatism clung.

Figure 7. Watchtower where Ancient Letters were found

The reason these letters were not delivered as intended, it has been hypothesized, was due to the mailbag being seized by guards at the Jade Gate, as Sogdian relations with the Chinese were difficult at times. Of the eight letters, all but one were still sealed, and five were in a sufficiently good condition to be dated. After being opened back in Europe and later deciphered by Sims-Williams, they were dated to probably AD 313 and would reveal Sogdian traders operating deep within China. The letters, among the only ones ever discovered that were written by Silk Road merchants themselves, represent a 'documentary collection altogether unique in the history of Sogdian commerce' according to Vaissière. In a wider context he adds that 'few documents can be said to have had such a significant impact on knowledge of fourth-century Central Asian history'. Their dating is based on one of the letters, which in part refers to the sacking of the Chinese capital two years earlier:

> And, sirs, it is three years since a Sogdian came from 'inside' [i.e. from China] . . . and now no-one comes from there so that I might write to you about the Sogdians who went 'inside', how they fared (and) which countries they reached. And, sirs, the last emperor, so they say, fled from Luoyang because of the famine, and fire was set to his palace and to the city, and the palace was burnt and the city [destroyed]. Luoyang (is) no more . . .

Significantly, the writer goes on to point the finger at those responsible, naming the plunderers as 'Xwn'—transcribed in Sogdian as 'Huns'. His passing reference has generated intense debate among researchers; while Vaissière highlights that here, for the first time, was 'the establishment of a long-suspected but never proven link between the Xiongnu of old Chinese sources and the Huns unleashed on Europe from [AD] 370'. He goes on to conclude: '[T]he Huns' invasions in Central Asia gave way to the sole domination of the Sogdians on the caravan routes of Central Asia'.*

---

*   Quoted from his essay in *The Silk Road: Trade, Travel, War and Faith.*

There was a different link, however, that was established by another letter. Four of the legible ones were to be delivered within the Western Regions, perhaps to the Indianized kingdom of Loulan, but the fifth letter was addressed to faraway Samarkand. For traders living in the Chinese capital, this link represented a distance of some 3,000 kilometres or eight months travel, proving beyond doubt the long reach of the Sogdian network. Since the climate of their homeland was not as dry as the Tarim, and their soil more acidic, few Sogdian documents have survived over the centuries. Even of those that have, many were destroyed following the Islamic conquests and conversions, after which Sogdians ceased to exist as a people, thus making Stein's discovery all the more valuable.

Other than their historical importance, these letters detail the type of goods being traded along the Silk Road. They also record several Indian words which Sogdians had incorporated into their language, including *caravan, letter, price* and *pepper*. These documents also bear testimony to the trials faced by immigrant Sogdians. Two of the letters were from a lady named Miwnay: the first to her mother Chatis (an Indianized Bactrian name), pining to return home, while the second was addressed to her husband. In the latter, she vents her frustration for being abandoned with her daughter far from home:

> My misfortune is this, (that) I have been in Dunhuang for three years thanks(?) to you . . . I obeyed your command and came to Dunhuang and I did not observe (my) mother's bidding nor (my) brothers'. Surely(?) the gods were angry with me on the day when I did your bidding! I would rather be a dog's or a pig's wife than yours!

Working along the Great Wall and its watchtowers, Stein was confronted with another discovery: an imposing fort standing ten metres high, with walls almost five metres thick at their base. From the abundant Chinese documents found here, it quickly became evident, as he described, 'that we had struck the site of that famous

"Jade Gate" at which we know that in Han times all traffic passing along the desert route was controlled'.

Finally, after completing his work along the Chinese *Limes* and driven out by the growing heat of the desert, Stein returned to Dunhuang—a shadow of its former self, now reduced to a dusty little town, but still home to the 'Caves of the Thousand Buddhas' (also known as Mogao Caves). A fellow Hungarian geographer, who had previously visited there almost thirty years earlier, had alerted him that the caves contained Indian Buddhist artworks; while Stein had recently learnt from a Turkic trader of a newly discovered cave supposedly full of documents. Although he didn't plan to excavate here, as it was an active pilgrimage site, Stein longed to see the cave art and, as he later wrote: 'The thought of the great store of old manuscripts awaiting exploration drew me back to the Caves of the Thousand Buddhas with the strength of a hidden magnet.'

A tablet later found in one of the caves recounts how in AD 366 a wandering monk:

> . . . resolute, calm, and of pure conduct . . . travelling the wilds with his pilgrim's staff, arrived at this mountain and had a vision of a golden radiance in the form of a thousand Buddhas. Thereupon he erected a scaffolding and chiseled out the cliff to make a cave.

Over the next 1,000 years, other monks would follow and hew out new ones into the rock face, some as simple living quarters or meditation cells. Others would be constructed as elaborately decorated temples, sponsored by rich and powerful patrons or sometimes by local merchants banding together to commission a smaller shrine.

After the last cave was dug in the fourteenth century, the complex came to comprise over 1,000 caves stretching along a stream for almost two kilometres. Approximately half of the caves are decorated, and in total they contain some 3,000 statues and murals, including three colossal images of the Buddha. The largest of these, housed in a cave that rises nine storeys, stands over thirty-five metres and is the third tallest such statue in the world. Adorning the plastered walls are paintings depicting *bodhisattvas*, sacred legends and saintly attendants, often with facial features and clothing distinctly Indian in origin. Many of the artworks are simply stunning in their execution and beauty; and have remained well preserved due to the absolute dryness of the walls and atmosphere. An inscription in one of the caves reads:

> Whenever faith exists it will not be altered by human affairs. Those who believe deeply in the Buddha consider it possible that when he arrives the wind and waves will be calmed. Thereby he will be welcomed to the Dunhuang temples and be worshipped forever.

Today, over 200,000 people visit the caves every year from across the globe. They come to admire and study what UNESCO's World Heritage List describes as 'the largest, most richly endowed, and longest used treasure house of Buddhist art in the world'.*

When he arrived, Stein found the complex had become a thriving centre of worship and the residence for holy men. He waited until after the annual pilgrimage to the caves was over and the thousands of visiting worshippers and monks had departed. Then he approached the self-appointed custodian of the shrine complex, a Taoist priest named Wang Yuanlu, who now devoted his life to its upkeep. Initially, he had come here as a discharged soldier and, after making the caves his home, eked out a living selling Taoist spells to locals. Seven years before Stein's arrival, the priest had stumbled upon the concealed doorway to a small chamber within a temple cave and found it crammed full of documents. Wang had initially alerted Chinese authorities to his find, who requested the

---

* UNESCO is short for United Nations Educational, Scientific and Cultural Organization. The caves were inscribed on its World Heritage List in 1987.

entire hoard be sent to the provincial capital. When funds were not available to transport the contents—upwards of 50,000 manuscripts and artworks—he was instructed to simply reseal the chamber instead. Stein would subsequently learn that the first time it had been plastered and painted over was around AD 1000, to create a safe depository for old documents or perhaps to safeguard its contents from the ravages of war.

Figure 8. The Hidden Library: small, high doorway to library is seen on extreme right with manuscript bundles in the foreground

With Jiang Siye's assistance, Stein convinced the priest to allow them access to this 'library' which he had fitted with a locked door after its discovery.* In Stein's five-volume expedition report titled *Serindia*, he later described what awaited him upon entry into a veritable time capsule:

> Heaped up in closely packed layers, but without any order, there appeared in the dim light of the priest's flickering lamp a solid

---

*   This chamber is often referred to as the Library Cave or simply designated Cave 17.

mass of manuscript bundles rising to a height of nearly 10 feet [3 metres]. They filled, as subsequent measurement showed, close on 500 cubic feet [14 cubic metres], the size of a small room or chapel being about 9 feet square [1 square metre] and the area left clear within just sufficient for two people to stand in.

The manuscripts were in eight languages, including Chinese and Kharosthi, the earliest of which would be traced back to being scribed in AD 406. Up until this time, the main method for writing languages other than Chinese in the Tarim had been Kharosthi, as also used by the Kushans, after which the script fell out of use. (Using Chinese was not possible because it employs characters rather than an alphabet and cannot therefore write the sounds of other languages.)

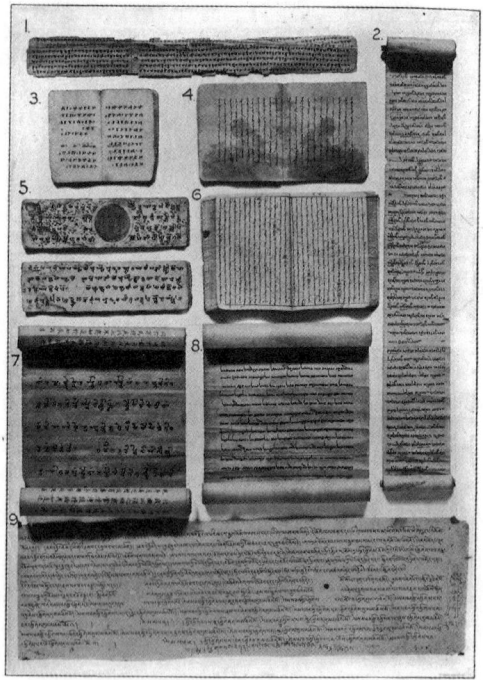

Figure 9. Manuscripts found in the Hidden Library:
written in various scripts including Sogdian (item 8)

It was abundantly clear to Stein that: 'Not in the driest soil could relics of a ruined site have so completely escaped injury as they had here in a carefully selected rock chamber . . .' But after a cursory examination of the piles, he found that many of the items had been poorly stored and were susceptible to further damage, including the exquisitely painted silken banners which had been used to drape temples and stupas with, as an act of veneration. Stein was, however, deeply impressed by Wang's dedication to the upkeep of the caves, crude though much of his restoration work was, and would later witness how he dutifully recorded donations received into a red book. The archaeologist's challenge now was to find a way of convincing the reluctant priest to part with as many items as possible, *all* of which were historically important—initially, for the entire lot, Stein offered forty silver horseshoes (worth about 5,000 rupees then). Desperate though he was to secure funds for the shrine's upkeep, Wang would not agree to releasing more than a portion of the library, and he was particularly reluctant to part with any Chinese scriptures or texts.

Through conversation, Stein learnt that the priest was an ardent admirer of Xuanzang, who had passed through Dunhuang centuries earlier on his return to China from India, a journey of some seventeen years, bringing back hundreds of Buddhist scriptures he had gone there to secure. Stein had genuinely adopted the travelling monk as his own patron saint, and spoke to Wang about how he had 'followed in his footsteps from India over ten thousand *li* across inhospitable mountains and deserts'. He drew parallels between Xuanzang's lone quest and his own to obtain sacred texts, only this time going in the other direction 'to allow Buddhist scholars in India and the West to benefit by them'. This connection was firmly established when, to their amazement, amongst the first batch of sutras inspected by Jiang Siye were found translations made by Xuanzang himself. It almost seemed as if the holy man were speaking to them from beyond the grave; and when Stein suggested to Wang that his own arrival here was somehow fated, the priest was convinced and consented to the library's contents being examined.

The 'black hole', as Stein described the chamber, was hurriedly emptied before he sorted through the piles of documents as best he could, although his inability to read Chinese meant having to rely heavily on Jiang Siye. Fortunately, as far as the artworks were concerned, Stein was well qualified to judge these himself:

> To my surprise and relief, he [Wang] attached little value to these fine art relics of Tang times. So I could rapidly put aside 'for further inspection' the best of the pictures I could lay my hands on at that first day's rapid search.

Then, after *much* cajoling over several days and nights, Stein finally convinced Wang to release a portion of the hoard for *one-tenth* his original offer, as he later reflected:

> When I now survey the wealth of archaeological materials alone that I carried away for this sum [equivalent to £130], the bargain may well seem great beyond credence.

The bundles were removed at night, without the knowledge of the other monks on site, and through this process some 9,000 documents and artworks were acquired, in total making up seven camel-loads of material. (Within years, other foreign archaeologists would follow and, just as controversially, 'purchase' many thousands of items for their own museums. On his third expedition, Stein would also acquire another five cases of manuscripts.)

Amongst the many scrolls Stein shipped back and were later transcribed was the prayer by the bridegroom quoted earlier, reciting his desire for acquiring many slaves. Around three-quarters of the manuscripts would simply prove to be copies of well-known Buddhist sutras—a way of acquiring merit for anyone having the words or image of the Buddha replicated. Yet even these are of some value as each scroll contains a footnote describing when, why and by whom it was sponsored, thus opening a small window into the lives of ordinary worshippers. One, for example, was by a government official promising to have a scroll copied out every month were he to attain promotion to sixth grade, and which would be increased to two rolls if it happened to be the fifth grade. Another commission by a nun named Tao Jung in AD 550 was perhaps more heartfelt:

> [Having] cut down her expenses in food and clothing, caused [this] section of the Nirvana Sutra to be copied . . . [to] influence others to their enlightenment . . . [such that she] might abide her present life in meditation, without further sickness or suffering . . . [given that] she did something evil in a past life . . . and was reborn in the vile estate of woman . . . If she did not obey the wonderful decree of Buddha, how shall she find repose?

To Stein's delight, other than the many copies of sutras, there were priceless items discovered amongst the documents as well.* One example was the earliest manuscript map of the stars known today from any civilization. Produced early in the Tang Dynasty, it depicts the night sky as seen by the naked eye from central China. Another was a Tibetan version of the Indian classic *Ramayana*, except this one was less moralistic than the original Indian version and concluded with a happier ending.

Stein's most important find, however, would prove to be the *Diamond Sutra*, the world's oldest-known and dated (AD 868) printed book—published 600 years before the Gutenberg Bible was first 'mass-produced' in Europe. It had been block-printed in Chinese characters on seven sheets of paper, which were then glued together forming a scroll almost five metres long. Regarded today as one of the world's great treasures, it has a magnificent frontispiece

---

* Through the International Dunhuang Project, established by the British Library in 1994, many of these items have been digitized and made freely available to all.

depicting Buddha preaching to the faithful. A line from one of its verses reminds readers that: '[The] happiness of one who writes this sutra down, receives, recites, and explains it to others cannot be compared.' On its conclusion, this priceless book notes that it was 'reverently made for universal free distribution'.

The magnitude and importance of the contents from the Hidden Library have been compared with the Dead Sea Scrolls (also found in a cave and preserved by the dryness of the surrounding desert). They continue to be intensely studied and appreciated across the world, although the people of China understandably remain aggrieved about the items removed. So what to make of Stein's actions? The answer depends on one's point of view, perhaps taking into account the state of affairs *at the time* with regards to protecting cultural artefacts in faraway places. Sinologist Arthur Waley, who worked on some of the material the archaeological explorer brought back, points out why the Chinese regard Stein nothing short of a robber:

> I think the best way to understand their feelings on the subject is to imagine how we should feel if a Chinese archaeologist were to come to England, discover a *cache* of medieval MSS [manuscripts] at a ruined monastery, bribe the custodian to part with them, and carry them off to Peking.

Stein's initial biographer, Mirsky saw his actions in a different light:

> [Stein's own account] is hardly that of a man who thought of himself as a 'robber' or 'bandit'. Only a man committed to the primacy of Western learning could write so fully, so honestly of what had transpired . . . There is no sense of guilt or of having been a party to sacrilege. How could he have foreseen what the attitude would be both in China and the West half a century later?

The artefacts Stein brought back were processed by experts in England, together with those from his first expedition, and about two-fifths have remained there. His later biographer Annabel Walker notes, however, that:

> Many of the items which Stein resurrected from the desert arrived in the West only to be buried yet again. Of the large Stein Collection at the British Museum, only a fraction is displayed . . . most have been stored in the basements where they were first unpacked . . .

And with regards to the controversy he generated, she reminds readers:

> It seems glib to condemn a man for acting in a way entirely consistent with the period in which he lived and the Western world in which he was raised.

Another person who has studied and written extensively about Stein, historian Susan Whitfield,* makes an important point about his involvement with the Hidden Library:

> Yet Dunhuang was not typical of Stein's work. It was someone else's find and did not require excavation, rather persistence, diplomatic skills and a small amount of money to acquire a part of the discovery. It has rather overshadowed his work further west which, in terms of its potential scholarly impact, was just as important.

The majority of items from Stein's first two expeditions were eventually shipped back to his employer, the (British) Government of India; but all items from his third were kept on the subcontinent as this trip was funded solely by India. Today, many of these artefacts are permanently displayed in two large rooms that make

---

* She was also Director of the International Dunhuang Project from its inception to 2017.

up the Central Asian Antiquities exhibit of the National Museum in New Delhi. (The remains of priest Wang Yuanlu, incidentally, lie undisturbed within a small stupa located in the grounds of the cave complex in Dunhuang.)

In the years after returning from his second expedition, many honours were bestowed on Stein. Foremost amongst these, and which he regarded as his greatest encouragement, was one of two gold medals presented annually by the Royal Geographic Society in London; the citation: 'For his extensive explorations in Central Asia, and in particular his archaeological work.' This honour represented the pinnacle for any explorer, and was conferred during an era when the society was the pre-eminent institution in the world with regards to geographical exploration. Amongst the other awards he received was a knighthood, and honorary degrees from both Oxford and Cambridge universities. For Stein, an Anglophile* and a confirmed bachelor who had devoted his life to scholarly work, such recognition was particularly special. Later, on the first page of his book, *On Ancient Central-Asian Tracks*—being a collation of his three expeditions traversing 40,000 kilometres over seven years—he would write: 'The years spent on hard travel in those little-known regions, difficult of access and trying in their physical features, remain among the happiest memories of my life.'

It was during his third Central Asian expedition, ending in 1915, that Stein found time to thoroughly explore the Pamirs. Having packed off almost 200 heavy cases with archaeological finds bound for Kashmir, he was retreating from the heat of the Tarim Basin ahead of summer. This time he followed sections of one of the greatest long-distance caravan journeys ever undertaken. It was made by a merchant named Maes (also known as Titianus), and it was from his account of a trek to China around AD 100 that Ptolemy had described the Stone Tower and where it was to be found. No written

---

* In 1904, Stein became a British subject after renouncing his Hungarian citizenship.

description of the trade route through the Pamirs would again be available for over a thousand years, not until Marco Polo's account. Yet Stein's attempts to locate this significant landmark have been treated as something of a side excursion by scholars later discussing his work, if they mention it at all—only one of his two biographers does, and then ever so briefly.

Stein initially headed into the Pamirs from Kashgar, the Han Dynasty's last western outpost, towards the Taun-murun Saddle sitting above the border post at Irkeshtam. Once on the other side, travelling down the Alai Valley, he arrived at a village named Daraut-Kurghan (or Daroot-Qurghan), all the while carefully observing the approaches to it, noting: 'Experience gathered elsewhere in the East had long before taught me the advantages of such study on the ground itself where questions of historical geography were concerned.' After consulting Ptolemy's work, he came to the conclusion—agreeing now with Henry Yule rather than Henry Rawlinson—that it was somewhere in this vicinity that the Stone Tower once resided. Was he right this second time? Only by retracing the ancient caravan routes and through a detailed examination of *Geographia* can we hope to come up with an answer.

PART THREE
PTOLEMY'S STONE TOWER

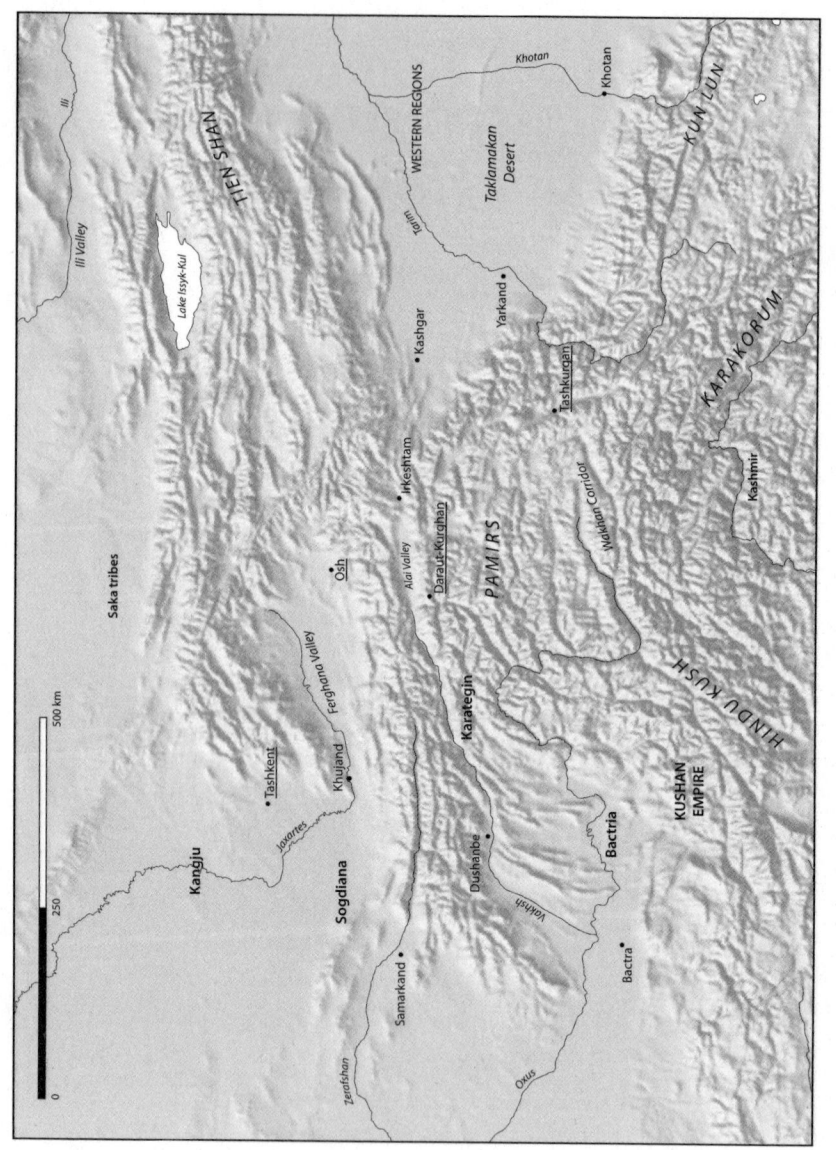

Map 4. Vicinity of the Stone Tower: with its four likely sites underlined

12

Ptolemy's *Geographia*

The quest to find the Stone Tower has gained momentum through the ages and, in the process, generated much 'spilt ink'—but to what purpose, one might ask? The answer lies at several levels but simply put, it was *the* most important landmark for travellers along the Silk Road. Both geographically and figuratively it represented the heart of the overland trade network, and was a halting place that Ptolemy referred to frequently in his *Geographia**. Of itself, this makes its search worthwhile and almost needs no further justification. Here, caravans moving between Europe and Asia would break their often long and arduous journeys to allow merchants and other travellers to rest, trade goods and take on provisions before continuing to the next stage.

In modern times, the interest in this Eurasian network has been steadily increasing ever since Stein and others initiated the concept of Silk Road Studies around the beginning of the twentieth century. The second phase of this scholarly field started gaining impetus in the 1980s, spurred on as Central Asia became more accessible to visitors across what was once Turkestan and which, until recently, had been split into Russian and Chinese halves. The western Soviet half then

---

* *Geographia* is the Latin translation of the abbreviated title of his text, originally written in Greek. The Stone Tower is *Lithinos Pyrgos* in romanized Greek and *Turris Lapidea* in Latin.

comprised the now independent five countries ending with *stan* (meaning 'land of'),* while across the Pamirs still lies the Chinese half represented by the massive but sparsely populated Xinjiang province. Tourists have recently begun travelling the length of this timeless caravan network in increasing numbers, seduced by its evocative images and historic sites, keen to experience its myriad of people and cultures. As a marketing tool, 'the Silk Road' phrase is frequently employed in a multitude of ways and across many countries, to the point where its historical legacy is now blurred by metaphor.

Described as the world's earliest highway, acclaimed cellist Yo-Yo Ma has gone further, labelling it 'the internet of antiquity'. In 1998, he founded the Silk Road Project, a not-for-profit organization which celebrates the living arts of peoples along this network. Four years later, his ensemble played at the Smithsonian Folklife Festival in Washington DC, an event which hosted well over a million visitors that year under the banner *The Silk Road: Connecting Cultures, Creating Trust.*

In a more permanent way, the International Dunhuang Project strives in its mission 'to make information and images of all manuscripts, paintings, textiles and artefacts from Dunhuang and archaeological sites of the Eastern Silk Road freely available on the Internet'. UNESCO, in particular, has worked hard to promote and institutionalize this second phase through a great deal of research and literature, including its initial ten-year project *Integral Study of the Silk Road: Roads of Dialogue* begun in 1988. To date, it has designated over a dozen Silk Road sites on its World Heritage List, although a possible listing of the Stone Tower still eludes it for want of proof.

Even before Ptolemy's time, from the shores of the Mediterranean all the way to the Greek colonies of Central Asia, the country and its settlements were relatively well known to the ancients, but eastwards from Bactria the geography became increasingly vague. In one of his maps—the one containing the Stone Tower—Ptolemy also stated the location for *over one hundred* towns and physical features, but the coordinates he left us were approximate at best, as will soon become

---

* Kazakhstan, Kyrgyzstan, Tajikistan, Turkmenistan, and Uzbekistan.

evident. If his midpoint of the Silk Road could be pinpointed, then this would certainly lead to other pieces of historical geography and cartography falling into place. Identifying a likely location would also allow future archaeological work at other sites in this vicinity to be more targeted, thereby increasing the chance of successful excavations and the discoveries that would surely follow.

Kang pulled his peaked cap closer around his ears and tightened his knee-length coat about his waist to ward off the morning chill. Yet he still felt the cold and tiredness in his bones. It added to his growing weariness from the responsibility that came with the title Sabao, which set him apart and somewhat alone as the leader of a caravan. More and more nowadays, during the long marches he found his thoughts drifting back to seasons gone by and the many trails taken. He stroked his almost-white beard, remembering well the times with his father and their blood relatives from the steppe, whom he saw less of now. Once the route through Ferghana had become safer and well-trodden he, too, had favoured it above others. After his father was crippled while taming a wild horse, there seemed little value in keeping the stud farm. So, he had moved the whole family into Samarkand, including his widowed daughter and her children, whose husband had been knifed in a dispute by a dry well deep in the desert. Their town, stretching along the wide and lush valley, was growing steadily and its many irrigation channels off the Zerafshan River had proved a boon for farmers. He had staked out his land at a good time, when its location along the caravan routes made the most of the plentiful trade during these peaceful times.

Although his books have survived, of Claudius Ptolemy the man almost nothing is known—what little there is must be inferred from his own writing, but this leaves no doubt as to his genius. 'He stands like a colossus astride the ancient world, and his influence is still felt today' according to antiquarian map authority R. V. Tooley, who goes on to add: 'His *Geographia* dominated the whole of the Christian and Moslem world for 1,500 years.'

J. W. McCrindle, while translating sections of *Geographia* for his text *Ancient India as Described by Ptolemy*, described him as 'a Mathematician, a Musician, an Astronomer and a Geographer . . . altogether one of the most accomplished men of science that antiquity produced'. But with this great stature came an inherent problem: Ptolemy's theories often went unchallenged, and his cartography remained unquestioned for centuries. So much so that he both inspired and misled Christopher Columbus into discovering America: The existence of both American continents was unknown at the time; after having consulted his work, Columbus serendipitously sailed west in the belief that he would find the riches of Asia when he next made landfall.

Neither the date nor place of birth for Ptolemy has ever been positively established. Born around AD 90, he was a citizen of the Roman Empire who resided in its Egyptian province and its capital Alexandria, located on the Mediterranean within the Nile delta. Founded centuries earlier by the conqueror whose name it bears, this city was second only to Rome within the empire; and home to one of the finest institutions of the classical world, the Great Library of Alexandria—thought to have contained almost 500,000 books at one stage. (It has been said that, if the Jews were the People of the Book, then the Greeks were a people of *many* books.) In this library, Ptolemy would have undertaken his research, drawing on 400 years of scholarship by other great Greco-Roman thinkers.

Nearby was the city's thriving port, the largest in the empire, from where all manner of goods emanating from the Silk Road were shipped to and from Rome. Not only was it heavily guarded, but all crew and passengers were scrutinized and required to hold passports to enter or leave the enclosure. Often their luggage was searched for texts; and if any new or foreign books or manuscripts were found, they were promptly confiscated and copies made out by hand. Eventually, a copy was returned to the owner while the original was added to the library's collection.

The Great Harbour, as the port was known, also gave Ptolemy direct contact with shipmasters and merchants, allowing him to check old information and incorporate new reports. Even before his time, at the start of the Christian era, it is estimated that at least one ship departed daily from Egypt bound for the East. They sailed to Indian ports and others further afield, including the islands and coastline of Asia. One can well imagine what a fascinating place and hive of activity the port in Alexandria was: ships of all shapes and sizes; the docks teeming with people from many lands, calling out to each other in various tongues; the smell emanating from baskets of fresh fish; while all manner of exotic goods were traded, as a variety of currencies changed hands.

Amongst Ptolemy's prolific works, two scientific treatises were particularly important. The first was his *System of Astronomy*, which set out his theories about the motion of the stars through the heavens. This treatise—commonly known as the *Almagest* (Greatest)—was so highly regarded in the Middle Ages and amongst the Arabs that it made older works on astronomy superfluous, and their manuscripts were no longer copied or read. In *Almagest*, Ptolemy also set down scientific principles which have long endured: For example, when delicate observations requiring precision are to be made, these should be repeated and taken over a period of time to reduce inherent errors in the data gathered.

As with all his work, Ptolemy's theories were built on others before him. In terms of geography, however, no other classic Greco-Roman text on this subject has survived other than the work of Strabo, as cartographer Lloyd Brown notes:

> Nor could any man anticipate that for the most part, the geographic heritage of the human race was to rest for more than 1,200 years in the writings of two men: Strabo and Claudius Ptolemy: one for furnishing the key to the past and the other a pattern for the future.

Yet there *were* other great scholars before them, and a wonderful illustration of the ability of their predecessors comes from reports passed down of the deliberations of another polymath Eratosthenes (c. 275–194 BC), who also served as chief librarian in Alexandria. More than three centuries before Ptolemy was born, he estimated the earth's circumference with great accuracy despite having only rudimentary tools available. On the face of it, his methodology was deceptively simple: Eratosthenes knew that on the summer solstice* the sun stood directly overhead a town named Syene (today Aswan) because it cast no shadow into a deep well there. On that same day, he measured the angle cast by the shadow of an upright object, perhaps a column or pole, to be one-fiftieth of a circle at noon in Alexandria. Using the old Greco-Roman measurement of length, he estimated that Syene lay 5,000 stades (790 kilometres) away on the banks of the Nile, and from the flow of this mighty river he believed it stood directly south. By applying the mathematics of angles known at the time and taking fifty times this distance, he determined the earth's circumference as 250,000 stades,† equivalent to 39,500 kilometres—the true figure is close enough to 40,000 kilometres.

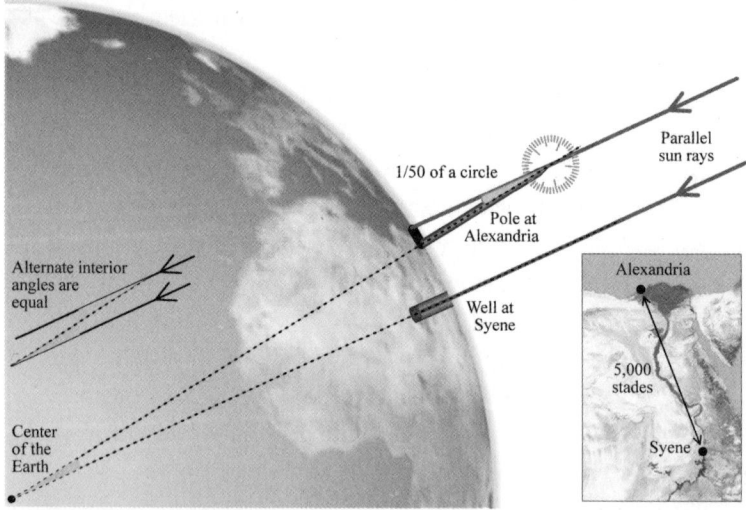

Figure 10. Eratosthenes's method for estimating Earth's circumference

---

*   The longest day occurring each year due to earth's tilting—late June in the northern hemisphere.
†   He increased it to 252,000 stades to make it neatly divisible by the 60 parts of a circle (later on, further divided into 360°).

However, there is a caveat to this seemingly astonishing result: the length of the stade is *not* certain and has varied over time and by region. In this book it is taken as 158 metres, equivalent to a conversion rate of 0.158 kilometres, although a range of values has been suggested up to 0.185 kilometres. At this higher end, Eratosthenes overestimated by sixteen per cent—still a remarkable effort considering it was made over 2,000 years ago and with rudimentary tools. Of course, this illustration is somewhat simplified: Eratosthenes's method was essentially correct, but his measurement contained a few estimates and errors which fortunately tended to cancel each other out. For example, the distance between Syene and Alexandria (roughly measured on foot, by a caravan, or perhaps a boat along the Nile) was underestimated but turned out to be close to the distance as the crow flies, which is what Eratosthenes had *intended* to measure.

In *Geographia*, Ptolemy departed from his predecessors by not concerning himself with the usual portrayal of people from various lands as related by their history, economy and culture—what we know today as *geography*. Despite the title of his text suggesting otherwise, he confined this work to a field that would later emerge as *cartography*; and after establishing its scientific principles, he set out to prepare a general atlas of the *oikoumene* (known world). He knew that by carefully applying astronomy and mathematics, it should be possible to accurately map the earth, just as he had already charted the heavens. All that was needed were the spherical coordinates—latitude and longitude—of every significant place and landmark, no different from what is required today.

Well before Ptolemy's era, a method to determine latitude had already been established, essentially by observing the shadow cast by the sun at noon during a solstice or equinox, similar to the technique employed by Eratosthenes. Measuring longitude between locations, however, was far more onerous in those times, as it involved noting the time that a lunar eclipse occurred at two places simultaneously. An example of such an eclipse occurred a few days before the momentous Battle of Gaugamela in 331 BC, when Alexander's army decisively defeated the Persians and changed the course of world history. A difference of three hours was observed then between Carthage and the battle site*, but even this measurement was only an approximation at best.

Ptolemy's main difficulty in preparing maps arose from the lack of reliable data for both coordinates. Latitudes were known for only a handful of major cities, while longitudinal measurements were practically non-existent. Nevertheless, locations that were already fixed, such as Rome, Alexandria and Rhodes, laid the groundwork for his maps. Other than these landmarks, it meant having to rely on the less accurate method of gathering information about distances and routes from travellers, such as sailors and those involved with military expeditions or merchant caravans. But herein lay his next problem, as often this data was not available either. Even when it was, accounts from travellers were typically unreliable and, through no fault of their own, they carried no measurement devices: neither compass nor timepiece. And although travel was well-documented along the Roman roads, for example, and for coastal shipping throughout the Mediterranean, routes to lesser-known regions were sketchy.

In his treatise, Ptolemy carefully explained the role that astronomy and other forms of data-gathering were required to play in map-making. He was in advance of his predecessors in two other ways: by setting down a clear methodology for how maps ought to be constructed; and by presenting the topography of the three then-known continents—Europe, Africa and Asia—in an extensive and detailed way.

Ptolemy was also the first cartographer apparently to formulate complex map projections depicting the earth's curvature. Ancient geographers had realized that since the earth is essentially a sphere, to map it without distortions, it should be drawn on a globe. However, because such a globe would have to be overly large to show sufficient

---

* Aurel Stein, in tracking Alexander, believed this site lay in present-day northern Iraq.

topographical detail, the only alternative was to draw maps on a plane or flat surface, such as a roll of papyrus, to the required scale. This meant projecting the earth's curvature onto a manuscript, which could only be done approximately and with difficulty. Ptolemy set out practical ways to achieve this, showing how different types of map projections could be drawn while dealing with the inherent distortions that arose from his methods, thus marking him as a true pioneer of cartography.

Although much of his work was original, Ptolemy gave credit where it was due. He especially noted that places and positions shown on his maps were mainly taken from the now-lost atlas of a geographer named Marinus of Tyre (c. AD 70–130), who probably died a decade before *Geographia* was prepared. Even though Ptolemy was often quite critical of his contemporary's work, nothing would be known of Marinus today if it were not for this acknowledgement; and Ptolemy went further to describe his efforts as done 'with absolute diligence'. In terms of their differences, significant though they were, it is clear from his text that Ptolemy expected readers would have access to *both* works and be able to compare them to make their own judgements.

Ptolemy's lasting innovation was his introduction of a system of well-defined coordinates. With such a grid in place, by specifying the latitude and longitude of locations, and describing physical features, a map could be reproduced accurately by fellow cartographers to any scale. This thrust is reflected in the original Greek title of his treatise *Geographike Hyphegesis*, which may be translated as 'Guide to Drawing a World Map'. His text comprises eight 'books' of varying lengths, covering three specific areas: First, there are instructions on how to draw the *oikoumene*, on both a globe and a flat surface. This is followed by an extensive gazetteer which makes up the bulk of *Geographia* (Books II–VII). In it he lists some 8,000 place names and their coordinates within the known world. Finally, there are long captions to accompany his maps.

In his last book, Ptolemy presented the known world in twenty-six regional maps, each with its own caption, comprising: Europe–

ten, Libya (Africa)–four, and Asia–twelve; the last set including the *Septima Asiae Tabula* (Seventh Map of Asia) which contained the Stone Tower. Some cartographers and historians suggest he did not publish any maps with his text, but more believe that Ptolemy did, as J. Oliver Thomson in his *History of Ancient Geography* points out: 'It seems likely that he would expect few readers with such bowels of brass that they would sit down to make their own atlas.' Nevertheless, according to O. A. W. Dilke writing in *The History of Cartography (Volume 1)*: 'The coordinates he gives are coherent on the whole and allow anyone to draw a map; but they are largely inaccurate and suggest that he did not verify either his own observations or those made by others.'

Given the infancy of cartography at the time and the pitiful lack of data available, it should come as no surprise that *Geographia* contained many errors. Despite this, and the fact that Ptolemy's view of the known world was similar to Eratosthenes's, he was one of the few geographers of that era to admit that the land mass extended beyond what was then known. But Ptolemy had a tendency to fill in these blanks with theoretical conceptions, even though his knowledge of faraway lands was sketchy. For example, he exaggerated the shapes of Africa and Asia, and disconnected the Atlantic from the Indian Ocean which he showed as enclosed by land. Yet he was the first geographer to correctly show the Caspian as an inland lake—something that Alexander the Great's army had realized while campaigning in Central Asia, as its waters were less saline than the Mediterranean, and it contained no ocean fish.

Ptolemy's biggest error stemmed from grossly underestimating the circumference of the earth. There is some reason to believe he may have initially agreed with the figure of 252,000 stades that Eratosthenes had first measured, but ultimately he revised it down to 180,000 (28,440 kilometres). This was too small, as we now know, but it did fool Columbus into believing he would not need to sail as far west, thus giving his expedition to the New World an added impetus. Of the geographer's errors, Tooley notes: 'This would not have mattered so much in a lesser man, but so great was the reputation of Ptolemy that his theories assumed an equal validity with his undoubted facts and were not seriously questioned for 1,500 years.'

The modern user or translator of *Geographia* also runs into difficulties. First there's Ptolemy's seemingly convoluted style of writing, with its many digressions and qualifications; as Thomson notes: 'His book is almost wholly unreadable and hardly meant to be read . . .' Then there's the long captions attached to the twenty-six regional maps in his final Book VIII, which confusingly employ a different system of coordinates altogether, as opposed to his gazetteer.* Finally, amongst the multiple translations and copies made since *Geographia* was first issued—more than fifty Greek manuscripts even before the fourteenth century—there are *many* disagreements. This is 'one reason why no satisfactory edition of the whole text of the work has been achieved in modern times' according to J. Lennart Berggren and Alexander Jones. The pair recently translated its theoretical chapters (omitting the gazetteer) into English—all translations from *Geographia* used in this book are by them, unless otherwise stated.

An ancient atlas without its maps, reduced to a mass of coordinates, will always be susceptible to corruption over time. Moreover, this one contained long-forgotten place names and complicated map-making instructions. And since *Geographia* is the only treatise on *cartography* to have survived from classical antiquity, no checking or clarification against other texts has been possible during the translation process. The earliest were from Greek into Latin, and then into Arabic with the flourishing of the Islamic empires. It was only centuries afterwards that some of its eight books were rendered into other European languages, with many fine copies being produced during the Renaissance. For English readers, the only

---

* Instead of continuing to use degrees, Ptolemy switches to presenting longitude as the difference in time from Alexandria, and latitude by the length of the longest day.

near-complete translation was by Edward Stevenson in 1932, but unfortunately it is riddled with errors and has been widely criticized.

After *Geographia* was first published, however, for more than a thousand years it seems to have fallen into oblivion and only rarely consulted, although it was used by Muslim cartographers in the ninth century. Fortunately, its text at least was rediscovered around AD 1300 by a medieval monk, who would hunt through old bookshops in the bazaars of Constantinople (now Istanbul) looking for works by classical writers. He had stumbled on rare books in the past, including a copy of Strabo's work, although he found it gnawed by rats. On learning of the possible existence of Ptolemy's manuscript, he set about finding a copy. After a great deal of searching, the outcome was recorded in the lengthy title of a poem: 'Heroic verses by the most wise monk Maximus Planudes on the *Geographia* of Ptolemy, which had vanished for many years and then had been discovered by him through many toils.' In fact, the monk eventually secured two copies but was disappointed to find that neither manuscript contained the maps described in the text. The poem goes on to relate how the Byzantine emperor exhorted the archbishop of Alexandria to assume patronage for recreating the missing world map and 'restore a likeness of the picture worthy of a king'.*

When the project was completed, a copy was presented to the emperor. It would have been a lavish work, prepared as a large-format map and ornately illustrated on parchment. The monk's find and subsequent labours were apparently the talk of Byzantium (or Constantinople, as it was better known as).

It is unclear, however, whether the preparation of the twenty-six regional maps was included in this project. Either way, Planudes would have been assisted by other monks from his monastery in reconstructing the map or maps. Importantly, Berggren and Jones

---

* There is some speculation that an Alexandrian draughtsman, Agathodaimon, had redrawn the world map much earlier than this time, by the sixth century.

point out that 'the success of their enterprise is proof that Ptolemy succeeded in his attempt to encode the map in words and numbers'. In fact, all later editions of *Geographia* would continue to present maps reproduced from the monks' initial work.

A hundred years on, when Constantinople was being threatened by the Ottoman Turks, an envoy was dispatched to seek assistance from two other Christian cities, Venice and Florence. He took the emperor's copy with him where it was transcribed and dedicated to the pope. Then, fuelled by the Renaissance, its dissemination began amongst the scholars and libraries of Europe. In this way many of Ptolemy's cartographical innovations were eventually adopted throughout the world, and a number are still in use today. These include his map projection styles, the use and layout of a gazetteer with coordinates, the map legends and conventions he employed, and even the orientation of maps with north shown on top. In time, *Geographia* would become the prototype for modern cartography, while map-making would be spoken of in terms of *before* and *after* the rediscovery of Ptolemy.

13

The Data

Amongst the many places that Ptolemy included in his atlas, he gave a specific location for the Stone Tower—an entry that continues to generate debate and controversy. All that we know of it originates from *Geographia*, which mentions it *ten times* in Book I and with a familiarity that suggests this was a well-known and established landmark. Frustratingly, though, Ptolemy fails to describe it further, not even a hint as to whether it was a settlement, natural feature, or perhaps a solitary man-made structure. After Book I, he refers to it just once more, in his gazetteer in Book VI when he details the Seventh Map of Asia but, on this occasion, he goes further and *reveals its coordinates*:

> The country of the Saka is inhabited by nomads. They have no towns, but dwell in woods and caves. Among the Saka is the mountain district, already mentioned, of the Komedai,
> of which the ascent from the Sogdiana lies in...................125° 43°
> And the parts towards the valley of the Komedai lie in.......130° 39°
> And the so-called Stone Tower lies in........................135° 43°*

On the face of it then, it seems a case of 'X marks the spot!' and locating his landmark ought to be a straightforward matter once the geographer's system of coordinates is understood and applied. But

---

* Translations from Book VI are by J.W. McCrindle.

this entry only throws up the first of many challenges. For although Ptolemy expressed both sets of coordinates in degrees, his basis for fixing longitude and latitude (which he states in this order) was different from what is used today.

Longitude was marked out as degrees east of the Fortunate Islands (present-day Canary Islands), which was the westernmost point known at the time. Ptolemy set his prime meridian here, starting at 0° and graduating the *oikoumene* over a span of twelve hours through to 180° east. This latter point sat just past where the Sera metropolis (Chinese capital) was thought to lie,* after which the *length* of the known world ended. The unknown half, *if* it were one vast ocean, would one day support the (erroneous) suggestion that by sailing west from the Fortunate Islands, a ship should reach China.

Latitude was designated in terms of degrees from the equator, just as it is expressed today; except that the main parallel was not the equator then, which was barely known, but one that passed through the Greek island of Rhodes lying 36° to its north. During this era, the *breadth* of the inhabited world was even less well understood than its length. Ptolemy set it from 63° north to a parallel 16° south of the equator, a span approaching 80° but still less than one-half of the length of the *oikoumene*.

Kang could see his sons, both strong young men, working busily to get the caravan moving as day broke. The younger one was calming one of the more spirited camels which had recently begun to give them trouble, while the older one haggled with a lately arrived itinerant merchant over the price of joining their caravan. He recalled, as if it were yesterday, placing honey in his boys' mouths and gum on their hands the day each was born—a Sogdian tradition to ensure their words would be sweet and money stuck in their grasp. After this season, there would be no reason not

---

*   Its location is debatable but probably was Luoyang since, during this Later Han period, the capital had been moved east from Chang'an.

to relinquish his caravan and title to the elder one. He would stay home and manage the trading business from their small warehouse—built outside the city walls so caravans could avoid its narrow lanes. Attached to the building was a large courtyard where pack animals were loaded and unloaded, and where their handlers and stable boys bedded down for the night. They would keep a watchful eye on his precious camels, which he also cautiously hired out to other merchants and travellers. The hirer always bore full responsibility for the animals and had to pay a compensation if one were injured or lost, as without the camels there would be no caravan trade.

Despite his best intentions in wanting to permanently record the site of the Stone Tower, there are multiple reasons why Ptolemy's coordinates, on their own, cannot locate it precisely. To begin with, they are simply not specific enough: Since *each* degree of his latitude represented 500 stades (79 kilometres), and for longitude around 400 stades (63 kilometres),* Ptolemy needed to specify the tower's geographical coordinates, which he had only revealed as 135° 43°, with more granularity, down to the equivalent of minutes and perhaps even seconds to pinpoint any such location.

Compounding the issue of longitude, he simply set its starting point—his prime meridian (0°)—as the Fortunate Islands, which itself was flawed as this group of islands span almost 5° of modern longitude. Heading east from there, Ptolemy started the coastline of Europe at 2½° instead of somewhere between 4° and 9°. Adding to this problem, his gross underestimation of the earth's circumference excessively distorted his maps in the east–west direction, making any longitude coordinate he gave approximate at best. And any distances he recorded are exacerbated by the uncertain value of a historical stade, as discussed earlier.

Complicating matters further, Ptolemy's stated longitude of 135° for the Stone Tower has some doubt attached to it, since he

---

* The east–west distance between lines of longitude *varies* with latitude; here it is approximated at Rhodes.

also *implies* in Book I, Chapter 12 that the figure could be 132° and, as Thomson points out, 'he does not explain the discrepancy, nor can anyone else'. Incidentally, this inconsistency is not immediately obvious in *Geographia*, but can be readily derived: the overall longitude from the Fortunate Islands to Sera is given as 177¼° and from the Stone Tower to Sera as 45¼°, thus their difference suggests the alternative figure of 132°.*

Doubts continue when, directly east of the Stone Tower on the border with China, Ptolemy described one last stop: a *hormeterion* (trading post or base, perhaps a caravanserai) 'whence traders start on their journey to Sera which lies in 140°'. By this stage, one could be forgiven for questioning the accuracy of Ptolemy's longitudinal coordinates (as obtained from Marinus) in and around these mountains. His gazetteer places the ascent to the Komedai at 125°, its valley at 130°, the Stone Tower at 135°, and the *hormeterion* at 140°—it all looks suspiciously like estimates set 5° apart for want of better information.

Other than longitude, there is also an irreconcilable issue with the latitude coordinate assigned to 'the valley of the Komedai'. Earlier in Book I, Ptolemy indicated it lay 'on the parallel through the Hellespont'† which he fixed at 41°, yet in Book VI he confusingly suggests it also lay at 39°—a significant departure of 1,000 stades (158 kilometres). The position of this valley is critical in locating Ptolemy's landmark because, as we will see in the next chapter, he stated in Book I that 'as one ascends the gorge [or valley], the Stone Tower comes next'.

So, was the valley of Komedai situated at latitude 39° or 41°? And was the Stone Tower's longitude 132° or 135°? A discrepancy of 2° in latitude and 3° in longitude equates to an area of some 1,200,000

---

* Similarly, as noted by Berggren and Jones, the difference in longitudes Ptolemy assigned to Hierapolis and the Stone Tower equals 65° whereas the land distance he gives amounts to only 60°.

† Hellespont refers to the narrow Dardanelles waterway in Turkey, separating Europe and Asia.

square stades (30,000 square kilometres)—larger than the island of Sicily—which almost reduces this search for a tower to looking for the proverbial 'needle in a haystack'.

The inadequacy of the many coordinates given in *Geographia*, particularly as one travels further east, was best summed up by Aurel Stein in his book *Ancient Khotan*, when he (and Henry Yule) warned against:

> . . . attempts to utilize Ptolemy's artificially deduced longitudes and latitudes for the determination of ancient localities in distant parts of Asia, where, as we know, the scantiness and unreliable character of the information at his disposal excluded the possibility of even approximately correct cartographic construction. The emphatic warning uttered by Sir H. Yule (*Cathay*, i. p. cli) on the subject of the deceptive nature of these definitions deserves to be taken to heart by students of Ptolemy's Asiatic Geography.

The classical scholar W. W. Tarn went even further in his criticism of Ptolemy in this regard, noting, with emphasis, in *The Greeks in Bactria and India* that 'the only value of his co-ordinates is to indicate that a place probably stood *somewhere* in that locality or to give very roughly its *relative* position'.

Other than these fundamental issues with Ptolemy's coordinate system, it is also clear from his text that *the way* in which he obtained information was problematic. Ptolemy learned of the Stone Tower from two sources, the first of which was contemporary sailors who frequented the bustling port of Alexandria. One such report that has survived antiquity is the *Periplus of the Erythraean Sea*—the 'sea' in this case being an expanse of water that included the Red Sea, Persian Gulf, Arabian Sea and Indian Ocean. This *periplus* (meaning 'handbook') was written a few decades before Ptolemy was born, and detailed the sailing routes, nautical distances and ports visited by an unknown Greco-Roman sea captain. By this stage, sailors and sea merchants were already making their way along the Spice Route to the coastlines of Arabia and India, and even further afield past the Golden Peninsula (Malaya) and onto China. Some of the information they garnered is captured in *Geographia*:

> From these people we have also learned other details about India, especially about the provinces and the more remote parts of this country as far as the Golden Peninsula and from that point on to Kattigara.*

Ptolemy goes on to give sailing directions and explain that, once there, Sera lay inland from the coast. If one were to now *return overland*, he once again makes mention of his landmark—the *only* time he does so from maritime reports:

> ... [there] is an unknown country that has reedy lakes ... They further [agree] that not only is there a route from [the Seres] to Bactria via the Stone Tower, but also to India via Palimbothra ...

The reedy lakes were presumably sections of the Lop Nor, where Stein had chanced upon the 200 Han-era copper coins lost by their owner along the dried-up lake bed. From this area, the caravan route through the mountains to India divided into two: the first went down the Indus Valley while the other followed the Ganges River, on whose banks stood Palimbothra (or Pataliputra, adjacent to present-day Patna). Centuries earlier, this city was the capital of the Maurya Empire (c. 320–180 BC) and one of the largest in the world. At the lower reaches of these two arterial rivers and their seaports began the Indian portion of the maritime Silk Road, the Spice Route.

The coastal sailors whose reports Ptolemy consulted were mostly nameless men, who *vaguely* knew of the overland Silk Road and its

---

* Kattigara's location is debatable: perhaps on the coast of southern China or Vietnam, or amongst the islands of Indonesia.

midpoint standing somewhere far inland. But Ptolemy's second source was altogether different, being traceable to a name whose account was undoubtedly more reliable, as he had reportedly visited the Stone Tower in person. The basis of *Geographia*, as we know, was the lost work of Marinus of Tyre, who in turn obtained much of his information about Asia from the trader named Maes Titianus and his caravan, as Ptolemy noted:

> Moreover, it was because of the opportunity for commerce that [the route] came to be known. Marinus says that one Maes, also known as Titianus, a Macedonian and a merchant by family profession, recorded the distance measurements, though he did not traverse it himself but sent certain [others] to the Seres.

The above passage is the *only* mention of Maes in classic texts. He was a wholesale merchant and possibly, like Marinus, lived in Tyre, then a Phoenician city in Syria. It was famous for producing the highly sought-after 'Tyrian purple' textiles which Roman nobility used to colour their silk garments. Assisted by commercial agents, probably Parthians, Maes and his family were importing raw Chinese silk for dyeing. By dealing directly with Seres, they were holding on to some of the profit that would otherwise be lost to various middlemen along the way. The journey undertaken by their caravan was completed around AD 100, after which its details were related to Marinus. Unfortunately, this is all we know of Maes since neither his actual account nor how Marinus used it for his own cartographical calculations has survived. Nevertheless, what little has been passed on by Ptolemy holds a unique and *much-analysed* place in the history of Eurasian trade networks. It represents the only complete description from classical antiquity of one version of the itinerary of the Silk Road which began from Hierapolis and the Roman border on the Euphrates River, before crossing Parthia and Central Asia to finally arrive in Seres.

Maes's caravan was highly unusual for two other reasons: During this period, both the Parthians and Kushans as key middlemen controlling trade between the Roman and Chinese empires, jealously guarded their monopolies and rarely allowed other merchants to cross their borders. For this reason, researcher Nathanael Andrade contends in his paper *The Voyage of Maes Titianos* that neither he nor his agents would have probably traded beyond the borders of Parthia. However, since according to Marinus they *did do so*, the prevailing political conditions must have been favourable for Maes to undertake such a risky venture in the first place. Most historians therefore date this epic journey close to AD 100 when the borders, particularly between Rome and Parthia, were relatively peaceful.

Another example of such an itinerary had occurred just three years earlier, when a Han envoy named Gan Ying was dispatched by Ban Chao, Protector General of the Western Regions, to the Roman Empire. But after travelling to the western border of Parthia, Ying decided not to continue after being discouraged by sailors' reports describing the difficult sea voyage to Rome. In Maes's case, as historian Max Cary points out, he would have needed powerful backing for his undertaking, which may have come from the Syrian governor. (Another possibility Cary suggests is that it came indirectly from the very top, from Emperor Augustus himself whose reign began in 27 BC—in which case Maes's caravan should be dated to a century earlier as some other researchers have hypothesized.)

The second reason for this caravan being unusual is the vast distance it covered, and the time involved: more than 10,000 kilometres, and taking some two years to complete. This is in stark contrast to the study by Valerie Hansen which concluded: 'The evidence at hand makes it clear that Silk Road commerce was largely a local trade, conducted over small distances by peddlers.' These everyday merchants would have moved regularly between towns and settlements, and their 'unremarkable' dealings probably would not have generated much external interest or written records.

When ancient geographers obtained reports from returning long-distance caravans, this information would have been passed on verbally from one trader to another, with the inherent likelihood of inaccuracies creeping into the written records made out at some later date. In the case of Maes's caravan, however, this information should have been more reliable, assuming he did travel to the Stone Tower (despite not going all the way to Seres, as noted in *Geographia*). Yet Ptolemy still records his predecessor's frustration in gathering information from such sources:

> [Marinus] himself apparently did not trust merchants' reports... For, [Marinus] says, these merchants do not concern themselves with finding out the truth, being occupied with their commerce; rather, they often exaggerate the distances out of boastfulness.

In terms of completing the expedition from the Stone Tower to China, he adds:

> But here also the circumstance that nothing else in the seven months' journey was deemed worthy of any record or report by the travellers reveals that the length of time is a fiction.

Maritime accounts from sailors probably suffered similarly, as Pliny the Elder had noted:

> The Seas are open to all, an infinite Multitude of Sailors have discovered all Coasts whatsoever; they sail through and arrive familiarly at every Shore; but all is for Gain, nothing for the Sake of Knowledge.

To prepare his maps, Ptolemy deserved better—instead of reports containing exaggerated distances and fictitious travel times, he desperately needed accurate data. He emphasized this requirement in Book I, in a chapter titled 'On the prerequisites for world cartography':

> But at the outset we think it is necessary to state clearly that the first step in a proceeding of this kind is systematic research . . . and that the inquiry and reporting is partly a matter of surveying, and partly of astronomical observation. The surveying component is . . . solely through measurement of distances; the astronomical component . . . from sighting and shadow-casting instruments.*

Neither Marinus nor Ptolemy had the crucial astronomical data at hand which might have allowed either geographer to sense-check statements from returning travellers. During this time, the 'matter of surveying' that Ptolemy wrote of was mainly conducted by way of overland travel but, in fact, amounted to nothing more than *crude* route surveys (maritime measurements were cruder still).† Caravans did not carry survey instrumentation during this era: no compass to gauge direction, nor astrolabe to measure latitude. As for longitude, it could only be estimated roughly by the travel time between stages since no portable timepiece was available to travellers then, for the simple reason that none had been invented. In the case of Maes's caravan, we know that the time taken from the Stone Tower to Seres was approximated and reported as a rounded figure in terms of *months*.

Even when caravan times were measured more diligently, the errors were still significant, as Edward Bunbury stressed in his two-volume *History of Ancient Geography*, where he also noted that the best the ancients could hope for, was to measure travel time in *days*. He demonstrated their handicap by citing an example of a march in Afghanistan by Alexander the Great's army: Eratosthenes

---

* The astrolabe was a sighting instrument then available to measure the inclination of celestial bodies, while a shadow-casting instrument could have been a gnomon or an upright object such as a pole.
† For more detail on conducting *accurate* route surveys, see my book *Mapping the Great Game*.

had set the distance his column covered from Kandahar to Kabul as approximately 2,670 stades, but a modern-day measurement by perambulator increased it by over one-third to 3,620 stades.* Similarly, in our earlier example when Eratosthenes estimated the earth's circumference, he had fixed the distance between Syene and Alexandria as 5,000 stades. His probable basis was information obtained from a caravan, yet the actual figure is more like 6,200 stades (the magnitude of his error depends on the length of the stade used).

Returning to Maes's caravan, Ptolemy criticized Marinus for not adjusting the reported time for rest periods and stoppages due to bad weather:

> However, we reduce according to the appropriate correction both the distance from that crossing of the Euphrates to the Stone Tower, which amounts (according to him) to . . . 26,280 stades, and that from the Stone Tower to Sera . . . 36,200 stades reckoned on the same parallel [through Rhodes]. For in the case of both journeys, [Marinus] has clearly not subtracted the excess resulting from diversions . . .

In adjusting for these diversions such as rest periods and stoppages, Ptolemy reduced the first part of the journey to the Stone Tower, but only by one-tenth to 24,000 stades 'because it has been measured in moderately sized parts that have been much travelled'. For the second leg, however, he pointed out that contrary to the reckoning by Marinus, Sera was not 'on the same parallel' simply due east.† Furthermore, he noted how merchants 'often exaggerate the distances out of boastfulness', thus concluding 'the length of time is a fiction'. His adjustment for this portion was therefore significantly greater:

---

* See Bunbury's Volume I, page 422 and footnote 6.
† Ptolemy set his latitudes as: Rhodes 36°, Sera 38°, Hellespont 41°, both Byzantium and Stone Tower 43°.

For these reasons . . . it would appear sensible here too, to diminish the number of stades added up from the seven months' itinerary, namely 36,200, to less than half. Let it, however, be reduced just to half, for this rough determination.

Ptolemy's approach here is telling: an arbitrary decision taken to simply *halve* an already rough determination.* In a similar fashion, as pointed out earlier, he had taken the span of the inhabited world which Marinus had set as 225° and reduced it down to 180° instead. According to Dilke: 'Ptolemy claimed to have accomplished this reduction by examining and comparing land and sea journeys, but it is likely that he relied more on guesswork than on sound calculation.'

Beyond the boundaries of Bactria, little was known of the countryside to the ancients with any certainty, so that by the time one approached China, as Thomson points out, 'the perversions of mapping are such that scarcely a name can be placed with any confidence'. And as to the Stone Tower itself, Bunbury states, 'But its nearer identification may be safely pronounced hopeless, from the utter vagueness of the *data* [his emphasis] furnished us by Ptolemy.' This is understandable given all the inaccuracies and approximations the great geographer had to contend with; and our examination thus far shows *beyond doubt* that his data, taken at face value, cannot pinpoint the Stone Tower. What then of Maes's *description* of the route itself—does this reveal the remaining information necessary? And what of the many scholars of ancient geography and cartography who, based on evidence currently available, have already pointed to a site where they believe Ptolemy's landmark resides—what are their views?

---

* Some researchers think Marinus may have misunderstood Maes, who possibly reported a *return* trip of seven months.

14

The Description

The actual route taken by Maes's caravan from Bactria to the Stone Tower, as detailed in *Geographia*, has been intensely analysed by researchers, particularly in the last 200 years. The *key passage* in Book I, Chapter 12 which describes this stage of the itinerary is reproduced in full below:

> Thence, the road to Bactra extends to the east, from there to the ascent of the range of the Komedai [the road goes] to the north, and from this range to the gorge that follows upon the plains [it goes] to the south. For [Marnius] places the northern and the westernmost parts of the range, where the ascent is, on the parallel through Byzantium, and the southern and eastern parts on the parallel through the Hellespont; this is why he says that [the route], though it leads pretty well straight east, tends to the *Notos* [south] wind. And apparently the fifty *schoinoi** from thence towards the Stone Tower incline to the north, for he says that as one ascends the gorge, the Stone Tower comes next, and from thence the mountains go off to the east and join up with the Imaon [range]†, which goes up from Palimbothra to the north.

---

* Ptolemy took one *schoinos* (plural: *schoinoi*) to equal thirty stades (4.7 km).
† Imaon corresponds in parts to Pamirs, Tien Shan and Himalayas.

Due to Ptolemy's 'complex' style, written in early Greek, there are understandably differences in interpreting this passage (above translation is by Berggren & Jones); therefore, three other English versions (by Yule, McCrindle and Stevenson) are also shown in the Appendix. Obviously, a great deal depends on this passage, yet a comparison of these translations—others exist in various languages—immediately highlights the first major problem encountered in turning to Ptolemy's description: literally, much is 'lost in translation'. These discrepancies are exacerbated by researchers using different texts of *Geographia* as their basis.* By the time Maximus Planudes rediscovered it, more than fifty Greek manuscripts had been copied out by hand, no doubt with many errors being inadvertently introduced by scribes over the centuries.

Having borrowed from a moneylender some years ago and with careful investment in merchandise, Kang's business in Samarkand had flourished and, with it, his standing in the community—now, no one spoke of his family's mixed blood. Their extended household with two dozen mouths to feed, including two servant girls, lived comfortably in rooms built above the warehouse. His many grandchildren gave him ample reason to stay home, where he could better supervise their education and keep a watchful eye on the older girls. The boys had already started learning the business; and there was so much for him to teach them, as the variety of goods that passed through their hands seemed to increase every season. There were various types of grain and spices to trade, and sometimes even exotic perfumes and gemstones; however, the business of onselling raw bales of silk to the Parthians remained their mainstay. Horses could be profitable, too, if a man knew how to pick out sturdy ones from a herd and then look after them well. This, he had learnt thoroughly from his father and grandfather, who had also counselled buying only the finest, which meant waiting until their caravan arrived in Ferghana. Then he

---

* Berggren & Jones used a Greek text, as did McCrindle, while Stevenson used a Renaissance Latin text.

would look for a quick sale after crossing the border before the desert took its toll on the steeds.

When caravans left Bactria and headed for China, the valleys they encountered offered few natural corridors across the Roof of the World, and many high passes still had to be negotiated through this immense knot of mountains. Travellers could choose from any one of *three* main routes to arrive at the Stone Tower, and then the *hormeterion*, before crossing the border. A *northern* route went up to Sogdiana first before travelling east along the Ferghana Valley; a *central* one went directly northeast through Karategin and the Alai Valley; while a *southern* route headed east along the modern-day Wakhan Corridor into the Pamirs. But, as historian Igor' P'iankov notes, 'none of these variants explains completely all of Ptolemy's data'. He contends, this is because Marinus had described *both* the northern and central routes leading to the Stone Tower, which Ptolemy had mistakenly combined into one, resulting in his seemingly confused description of the actual route. According to P'iankov, who has travelled through the region, this 'is the key to deciphering all of Ptolemy's data on [this] section of the route'; and on this basis he, too, attempted to identify the lost landmark.

In fact, from the data and description offered by Ptolemy, several locations have been proposed for his Stone Tower over the centuries. Of these, *four sites* have emerged as the most likely contenders, despite the many anomalies contained in *Geographia*. They have been either proposed or championed by various scholars—unfortunately, too many for the views of everyone to be reviewed in this book.

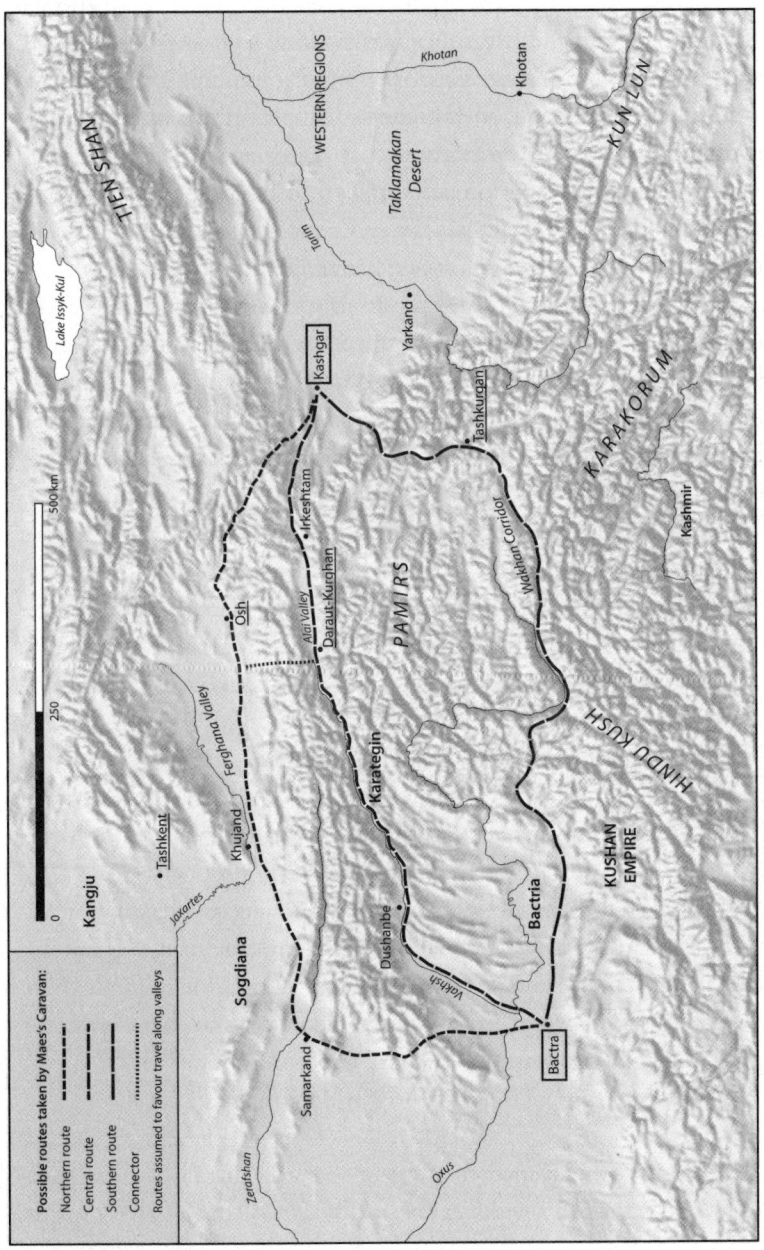

Map 5. Maes's Caravan: showing main route options from Bactria to Kashgar

The theories put forward by Aurel Stein, however, deserve special attention and for good reason: He visited all four sites—as well as many others—something which few others accomplished. And he understood this region from a practical and historical perspective like no other before or after him; ample evidence of which comes from his expeditions and multi-volume reports. Prolific author on Asia, Owen Lattimore, described Stein as 'the most prodigious combination of scholar, explorer, archaeologist and geographer of his generation'.

While leading his own caravan through Central Asia, Stein retraced the journeys of famous travellers who had passed before him, including Alexander the Great, Marco Polo and Maes Titianus. With regards to the latter's caravan and its halt at the midpoint of the Silk Road, Stein was able to revisit the question surrounding its location during his third expedition. In his three-volume report *Innermost Asia*, he finally settled on:

> [The] vicinity of Daraut-Kurghan as a very likely location for the famous 'Stone Tower' . . . The topographical facts here noted fully support the conclusion, first indicated by Sir Henry Yule, that the route from Bactra to the capital of Seres . . . led up through Karategin and the Alai valley.

Stein's conclusion was based on his on-the-ground observation that:

> [The] certain identification of the 'mountain country of the Komedai' which the essential passage of Ptolemy mentions on the line of the route, makes it quite certain that the route led through Karategin. I have already had occasion to show 'how Sir Henry Yule, by chain of sound critical reasoning, had been led to Karategin, as the probable position of the Komedai'.

The Komedai mentioned by Ptolemy refers generally to the Saka tribes who occupied a wide region north of the Oxus River. Towards its upper reaches near Bactria, a major tributary joins it from the northeast, known today as the Vakhsh, and is one of Tajikistan's primary rivers. Following this branch upstream along the *central* route, a traveller enters the Karategin region (also known as the Rasht or Gharm Valley) before the Alai Mountains begin towering over the narrowing floor of the Alai Valley (or 'gorge' according to Maes/Marinus).

Stein believed this was the area Ptolemy referred to in his key passage quoted earlier, as 'the range of the Komedai' from where 'one ascends the gorge' to arrive at the Stone Tower, thus concluding that it lay in the vicinity of Daraut-Kurghan. Archaeologists have uncovered stone foundations of large structures nearby, thought to be the remains of a settlement from Kushan times and earlier (second half of the first century BC), which go some way to supporting his theory. The site's Perso-Turkic name roughly translates to a 'tower at the gorge', and on this subject Stein went further, pointing out:

> This location is confirmed on the one hand by finding the same ancient name in the form *Chii-mit'o* applied by Xuanzang to a territory in a position exactly corresponding to Karategin, and on the other by the application to the same of the name *Kumedh* by early Arab geographers.

Daraut-Kurghan, today a small town of some 5,000 inhabitants, lies in southern Kyrgyzstan at an elevation of almost 2,500 metres.* Nestled in the Alai Valley, it sits on a road that runs northeast from Dushanbe (capital of Tajikistan) for 550 kilometres towards the Chinese border post at Irkeshtam. This post, according to Stein and others, represents Ptolemy's *hormeterion*, while the town of Daraut-Kurghan lies some 165 kilometres before it along this road.

A Roman chronicler Ammianus Marcellinus (c. AD 330–400) mentioned the Stone Tower in passing in his partially extant work commonly known as *Res Gestae* (he also made reference to the

---

* Its modern-day coordinates are 39°33' N, 72°12' E.

Great Wall and described the invasion of Europe then underway by the Huns). His text represents the penultimate major account of the ancient Western world which has survived from antiquity, although thirteen of his thirty-one books have been lost during the intervening years. In describing the provinces of the neighbouring Persian kingdom, while clearly making use of Ptolemy's work (Book VI, Chapter 13), he wrote:

> Next to these are the Saka, a tribe of savages, inhabiting a rough country rich only for cattle, and hence without cities. It is overhung by the mountains Ascanimia and Komedai, along the base of which and through a village, which they call Stone Tower, a very long road extends, which is the route taken by the traders who journey from time to time to the land of Seres.*

His reference to the Stone Tower being a 'village' (others see it as a 'town') may be important given that Marcellinus wrote within 250 years of Ptolemy, and his is the earliest *additional* information we have about this landmark. Scant though this is, it is likely that Marcellinus had access to other long-lost texts or maps describing the Stone Tower; and his record supports Stein's view of this halting place representing a settlement rather than a natural feature or man-made structure.

More recently, in his 2005 paper discussing *la caravane de Maes Titianos*, Paul Bernard carefully reconstructed and mapped the probable route of this epic journey all the way from Hierapolis in Syria to the Sera metropolis.† His placement of Ptolemy's landmark at Daraut-Kurghan concurs with Stein, Thomson, P'iankov and others—in fact, Daraut-Kurghan is the most widely accepted site for the Stone Tower by modern scholars.

---

*   Translated by J. C. Rolfe in *Ammianus Marcellinus (Vol. II)*.
†   Bernard did not place Sera at Luoyang, as others have, but at Wuwei (some 750 km southeast of Dunhuang).

Recently, however, after the publication of new material, doubts have been cast about this being the probable location, as we shall soon see. Of course, there is always the possibility that there was more than one Stone Tower located on other branches of the Silk Road, which could explain some of the confusion surrounding this subject. However, it is the one which Maes's caravan halted at, and which Ptolemy subsequently described, that is central to our search since only by finding *this* tower can other lost sites in *Geographia* be identified.

So, what of the three remaining locations most frequently suggested by other scholars? Stein, for one, had initially agreed with Rawlinson, as mentioned earlier, in locating the landmark at Tashkurgan—whose name translates as 'stone fort'. Yet there is certainly more than one settlement in Central Asia with this name, so this link, taken on its own, is hardly convincing. This town, by the way, was where the Sogdian trader Nanai-vandak was rushing to along today's Karakoram Highway when he left graffiti carved on a rock, as described earlier, expressing his desire to see his 'brother in good health with joy'.

If Tashkurgan, rather than Daraut-Kurghan, was indeed Ptolemy's landmark, this would imply that Maes's caravan took the *southern* route to China instead of either the central or northern ones (in which case it may have entered the Tarim through Yarkand rather than Kashgar). McCrindle, however, disagreed with this theory as he believed: 'Of the three routes, the itinerary of the Greek merchants could only apply to the 2nd [central] or 3rd [northern]'. Thomson also dissented, noting that 'it can hardly be, as it is not reached from the gorge of the Komedai'.

But Harry Falk has recently made a renewed argument for Tashkurgan. He specifically discounts Daraut-Kurghan, describing Stein's choice as 'simply guesswork', adding:

> Stein's paper was so influential that this supposed Alai route entered maps and even received the status of a 'caravan road'. On

the contrary we base own reflections on the observation that not a single traveller up to the 19th century can be named to have taken the full way through the Alai on a way from Dushanbe to Kashgar.

He goes on to point out that Stein was perhaps unaware Yule had, in fact, changed his mind about Karategin, later placing the Komedai further *south* of this valley, which would favour Tashkurgan instead. The names and itineraries of the nineteenth-century travellers Falk refers to have been documented by Middleton and Thomas in their book *Tajikistan and the High Pamirs*. They mapped the trails of over two dozen explorers through the Pamirs including, Russians, Germans, British and native Indians (the so-called Pundits, who were secretly dispatched by the Survey of India).*

Most of the early survey and mapping of these routes on the Roof of the World was undertaken during the 1800s. In 1970, however, a husband-and-wife team joined one of the last true caravans in the Pamirs on a trek through Afghanistan's Wakhan Corridor. Roland and Sabina Michaud, both photographers, published their experience and stunning pictures in *Caravans to Tartary*. The pair accompanied five Afghani-Kyrghyz caravanners leading a string of seventeen Bactrian camels, loaded with goods which they intended to trade with remote settlements lying along the banks of the Panj River (main tributary to the Oxus/Amu Darya). Twice a year their caravan made this 400-kilometre round-trip, turning back just before the Chinese border, and always travelling midwinter. Although this timing meant having to endure harsh conditions, the sub-zero temperatures allowed them to travel on the valley floor and cross the frozen river whenever necessary, rather than negotiate the treacherous mountainsides. Unknowingly, the Michauds recreated part of the journey from Bactria to Tashkurgan that Maes's caravan

---

* For more details, especially about the Pundits, see *Mapping the Great Game*.

might have travelled, but only *if* he had chosen to take the southern route as Falk suggests.

Falk began his 2018 study of *The Five Yabghus of the Yuezhi* by posing the question: 'how a tribe of nomads could afford to finance war with mighty opponents in the west and south in northern India over such a long time and over such extended regions'? The answer, he explains, was by each tribal division controlling a portion of the lucrative Silk Road trade between Bactria and the Tarim Basin, which they had dominated decades before their eventual unification by Kujula Kadphises and the emergence of the Kushan Empire.

By carefully comparing Ptolemy's text with the geography of the Pamirs, while drawing on material from early Chinese texts, Falk makes his case for Tashkurgan being the Stone Tower, noting that: 'Goods from China would arrive there, and goods from India could be deposited there, wherever their final destination.' Middleton and Thomas agree with him, and supporting their argument is another study in 2014 by a team from the Max Planck Institute for the History of Science led by Irina Tupikova. Interestingly, her team's approach did not follow the usual textual analysis of *Geographia* taken by most other researchers. Instead, they brought a fresh perspective to our riddle by employing a sophisticated cartographical technique which they described as 'the application of spherical trigonometry for the recalculation of Ptolemy's coordinates'. Although their methodology is beyond the scope of this book, their finding is clear enough: After resolving distances and locations along the Silk Road *beyond* the Stone Tower, as contained in *Geographia* and its Eighth Map of Asia centred around the Tarim, they concluded that 'this famous landmark of Ptolemy can with great probability be identified as Tashkurgan'.

Whether their theory is correct or not, there is another inescapable outcome from the work of Tupikova's team which, as they stress, starts 'with the following indisputable statement: Ptolemy put a position on his map only relative to another one, which we call a reference point'. Based on his data, their mathematical 're-mapping' relies on shifting his locations about this reference point. Thus, even if a *single* landmark such as the Stone Tower could be identified with certainty as *the* reference point, then many others would also fall into place—reinforcing the importance of finding Ptolemy's landmark to the study of ancient geography and cartography of this entire region.

The third site suggested by some scholars is Tashkent, today the largest city and capital of Uzbekistan, whose name translates as 'stone castle' in Turkic. Located just beyond latitude 41° N, it sits close to Ptolemy's designation of 43° and offers the best latitudinal match of all the four sites. On this basis the Arab polymath al-Biruni, who was born at the end of the tenth century and lived during the Islamic Golden Age as one of its greatest intellectuals, nominated Tashkent as the Stone Tower. Centuries later, McCrindle agreed with him, but neither he nor others have offered anything more substantial beyond these two reasons: similarity of name and closeness of latitude.

The fourth possible site lies by the city of Osh in Kyrgyzstan. In the mid-nineteenth century, geographer Carl Ritter, in his monumental work of twenty-one volumes,* placed Ptolemy's landmark here. Although explorer A. E. Nordenskiold did not advocate for any specific location in his *Facsimile-Atlas to the Early History of Cartography* published soon afterwards, he believed it was 'not a tower, or a town, but a mountain'. At the turn of this century, in his 2001 article attempting to decipher 'the incomprehensible Central Asian map of Ptolemy', archaeologist Claude Rapin agreed that it was not necessarily a settlement or man-made structure. Rather, he also believes it could be a natural feature and proposes a small mountain in Osh known by various names including Takt-e-Suleiman (Throne of Solomon), but he did not go much further in justifying his choice.

---

* Written in German—here, as referenced by Yule in *Cathay*... Volume I, page cxlix.

The Description   171

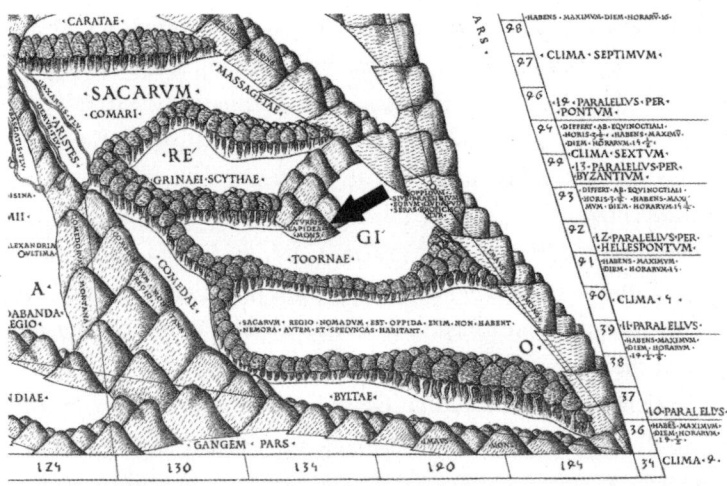

Figure 11. The Stone Tower (*Turris Lapidea*, arrowed): Depicted as a mountain (top, detail shown) versus a man-made structure (bottom, full map) at coordinates 135°/43°; from two recreations of Ptolemy's Seventh Map of Asia dated 1490 and 1620 respectively

In the West this mountain is often referred to as Solomon's Throne but is locally known as Sulaiman-Too (*too* means mountain in Kyrgyz). My article of 2015, titled *The Location of Ptolemy's Stone Tower: The Case for Sulaiman-Too in Osh*, agreed with Rapin but took an altogether new approach in advocating for this site, which this book now discusses in a fuller way. This 'mountain' is, in fact, a cluster of five rocky peaks that dominate the city of Osh located at the head of the Ferghana Valley. It is from here that Maes's caravan possibly used the Terek Pass to finally cross the mountain ranges and arrive at the Chinese border.

Whichever of these four probable sites ultimately proves to be the Stone Tower, if one relies solely on Ptolemy's *Geographia*—remembering no alternative text exists—it should be clear by now that the *data* contained in it is wholly inconclusive, and the *description* is not definitive either. This conclusion of itself is a *key* finding, not least because almost every researcher to date has relied mainly on an examination of *Geographia*—yet such an approach simply cannot succeed. Perhaps the best 'proof' of this assertion comes from the wide disagreement seen over time between so many eminent geographers, historians and cartographers. Moreover, if, as Marinus states, he had such little faith in the reports received from merchants—which contained exaggerated distances, fictitious times and were second-hand at best—there seems little value examining in minute detail the route taken by Maes's caravan as described in *Geographia*. And one wonders whether any amount of recalculation of Ptolemy's coordinates, no matter how sophisticated, such as those performed by the team from the Max Planck Institute, will ever produce a definitive answer. So where does that leave us—is this an impossible task?

15

A New Approach

In our quest to find the Stone Tower, the efforts to date of such a wide range of scholars—historians, geographers and cartographers—have proven invaluable in narrowing this search down to four solid choices. The sum of their knowledge over the centuries provides a sound platform to build on, while setting the scene for a fresh approach. It is worth noting, however, that in almost every case the location advocated by each one was done so while undertaking research with a wider focus, rather than looking at this problem exclusively. Unlike Stein, most did not have the opportunity to visit these sites either, as some are geographically inaccessible; while for outsiders, parts of Central Asia have often remained politically isolated. Despite these challenges, by overlaying the data and description given in *Geographia* with some 'outside the box' thinking, it may be possible to find a solution to our riddle.

To start this process, what is first required is a robust set of criteria. Then it becomes a matter of evaluating each site against these, before deciding on the best match. In terms of determining what these criteria should look like, the key question is this: Once the Silk Road had begun functioning, what were the essential requirements that such a prominent caravan stop would have needed to satisfy?

From Samarkand the route was an easy one, and even after that, other than through the high passes, the road had become safer and well-regulated by the Chinese. Unlike the Parthians, they let foreign merchants across their border and into their bazaars—only after paying taxes and bribes of course, from which there was never any escape. More caravanserais were springing up along the trails, with brisk trading at the bigger towns where there were good profits to be made. Kang's people were partnering better with the Kushans now, who were treating them almost as equals—begrudgingly, though—making good use of their reading and writing skills, as well as their ability to drive a hard bargain. Their southern neighbour still controlled the road to the rich ports of India, but the Tarim was opening up to the Sogdians. Some of them had even started moving out there with their families, settling as far as the big lake in the desert. Whenever his caravan passed through the oasis towns, they always came out to meet him. Later, they eagerly sought news from home while he and his sons dined with them—the fruit and wine from this region could not be bettered. But they knew to drink the wine sparingly, as the march between oases was long and hard, and their thirst would be desperate by noon. Sometimes he noticed the lady of the house quietly appraising his unmarried younger son as a possible son-in-law. For his part, Kang faithfully carried their letters back to relatives, loaned them money at a reasonable rate if asked, and gave families safe passage with his caravan when they wished to return home.

Choosing the *first* of our criteria poses no difficulty, as Ptolemy had made abundantly clear: the Stone Tower was on a major caravan route close to the crossover point into (and out of) the western extreme of China. We have already established the three main options available to Maes's caravan to reach the Stone Tower from Bactria. There was a northern route along the Ferghana Valley, a central one through Karategin, and a southern route via the Wakhan Corridor.

In fact, there was a fourth option also available, which involved going even further north past Tashkent until the steppe was encountered, before turning east along its grasslands towards the Ili Valley. This route avoided the twin dangers of the Pamirs and Taklamakan altogether, by circling north of the Tien Shan Mountains before turning south and passing through the so-called Dzungaria Gate to finally arrive in Dunhuang. Although this Eurasian Steppe Route was easier in some respects, it meant having to travel *much* further; and, just as importantly, caravans using this trail were susceptible to being plundered by the northern barbarians, which would have made this option decidedly less attractive. Even passing between these volatile tribal confederations was hazardous, as described by a Protector General in the *Hanshu* while discussing the inter-rivalry between the Xiongnu, Wusun and Kangju:

> Likewise they keep a watch on one another; and if they see a suitable opportunity, they then send out troops [against each other]. If they unite, they are incapable of enjoying each other's friendship or trust; if they are split apart, they are unable to make subjects of one another.

Travelling in the other direction from China towards the Stone Tower would have been no different. Once the Han established the Western Regions, the route from their capital through the Gansu Corridor was made safe for caravans right to the western edge of the Tarim. After this, they, too, had no alternative but to cross the mountains before negotiating the difficult paths down through the valleys to arrive at the halfway mark. Unlike the Steppe Route, however, this northern route to Ferghana had been secure ever since the Han had dominated the Xiongnu from 51 BC onwards, after the reigning shanyu had made peace with them and acknowledged their superiority.

Returning to our first criterion, although all four sites sat on this trading route, Tashkent is a poor match in terms of its distance from the Chinese border. Travelling between these two points by car today, it is over 650 kilometres away, whereas Osh and Daraut-Kurghan are less than half this distance from the border (Tashkurgan, of course, lies just within China). For a caravan averaging say twenty-five kilometres per day, this could have added an extra two weeks or more to its journey. We know from *Geographia* that Maes's caravan definitely left from Bactria when it headed for the Stone Tower and Seres, so halting at Tashkent would have involved a significant detour. This observation, coupled with the lack of any other substantial reason offered by scholars for Tashkent, makes it the least likely choice as Ptolemy's landmark.

Like our first criterion, the *second* is also straightforward: the Stone Tower was a clearly identifiable and permanent landmark. It would have needed to be for caravans to locate it and return here unfailingly. For this criterion, Sulaiman-Too is a standout candidate, as it is the only *permanent* landmark amongst the four (the other three being settlements were subject to human activity). The highest of its five peaks stands 191 metres above ground level.* Its irregular oval-shaped base covers an area of eighty hectares, measuring approximately 1,660 by 820 metres at its longest and widest points respectively. This collection of peaks has an impressive profile that can be seen from a long way off, particularly by a caravan coming up the flat Ferghana Valley from Bactria, as they stand well clear of the surrounding hills and mountains. Back then, none of the other three sites could be identified from afar as easily, since none had features which dominated their skyline in a similar manner.

---

*   Its height above sea level is 1,175 metres; while the mountain's precise coordinates are 40° 32' 23" N, 72° 48' 23" E.

Figure 12. Two ariel views of Sulaiman-Too from the north and south

Unlike a settlement or solitary man-made structure, Sulaiman-Too was not susceptible to being razed to the ground after violent conflict—conquerors of this region were known to dismantle whole cities at times, 'brick-by-brick'. But in any case, it is not certain whether any significant settlement or man-made structure, such as a citadel or tower, was present in the vicinity of either Tashkurgan or Daraut-Kurghan during Ptolemy's time. At Tashkurgan, sitting atop a nearby hill today are the remains of a large stone fortress, but this was built hundreds of years later, possibly in the sixth century. Perhaps of more significance are the stone foundations which have been unearthed near the village of Daraut-Kurghan, as mentioned earlier, and which archaeological dating places around the Kushan period or even prior to this. It is worth noting, however, that in his *An Historical Atlas of Central Asia* Yuri Bregel does not show any major archaeological sites at Daraut-Kurghan, or anywhere else nearby along the central route for that matter.

A *third* criterion hypothesizes that merchants would have favoured a route minimizing the 'cost of passage' for their caravans while maximizing their safety. The Silk Road was a *network* of routes, allowing caravan leaders flexibility in choosing the optimum trail depending on several prevailing factors at the time, including weather, geopolitical and economic considerations. The Stone Tower became *the* stopover point because it was favoured by a large number of caravans (even as others chose to go elsewhere for a variety of reasons). Two factors that determined cost of passage in such cases are distance travelled and time taken, both of which are directly influenced by the degree of difficulty travelling in a region of extreme topography and weather conditions. Such obstacles could also impact the physical safety of the caravan itself, as did the obvious threat from banditry, and were prime considerations in the final choice of the route taken by the caravan leader.

Applying this particular criterion, the northern route, although somewhat longer, would have been more favourable than either the central or southern routes, since the wide Ferghana Valley offered an easier passage through well-settled areas. (The final crossover through the mountains into the Tarim Basin was just as challenging for all three routes.) One logical predictor for the degree of difficulty negotiating mountain trails and the intensity of snowfall experienced is height above sea level. In our case this turns out to be: Tashkent–455 metres, Osh–963 metres, Daraut-Kurghan–2,469 metres, and Tashkurgan–3,094 metres. Due to their significantly higher elevations, the two latter sites experience more snowfall, again making them less likely choices as major caravan stops, particularly if they attempted to operate all year around. A satellite picture of this region taken by NASA in November (2003), before the onset of winter but already with high levels of snowfall present, illustrates this well. This photograph from outer space also shows the passage from Bactra to Osh and onto the Tarim as being the least hampered by snow compared to the other routes. Inclement weather here poses a constant threat to travellers; who would be wise to heed the cautionary advice offered in such terrain: *Mountains have a habit of making their own weather.* No doubt, caravan leaders were well aware of this as they endeavoured to cross the ranges in the least possible time.

Figure 13. NASA satellite image showing snowfall levels in Pamirs
(place names have been superimposed by author)

In terms of this third criterion, based on snowfall levels, Falk again discounts the central route proposed by Stein and others:

> But there is a serious reason which can explain why caravans seem to have neglected this Alai route. In comparison to the

plateau and the southern slopes of the Pamir, including the Wakhan, the Karategin-Alai Valley receives four times as much precipitation. Snowfall can set in at any time from August onwards . . . When the spring sun melts the snow the water makes long passages unusable.

Stein was aware that the area around Daraut-Kurghan experienced heavy snow, which closed the route to caravans for a number of months every year, but he also noted that it resulted in better pasture, which may have made up for some of this handicap:

> On the other hand precipitation, mainly in the form of snow, is far greater in the Alai valley than on the Pamirs, of which extreme aridity is a striking feature. The result is that the Alai valley has a steppe vegetation far more ample than that of the Pamirs . . . The abundance of grazing was bound to be appreciated by caravans, particularly those coming from the arid valleys on the Kashgar side . . . The route remains open for laden animals, including camels, during eight or nine months of the year.

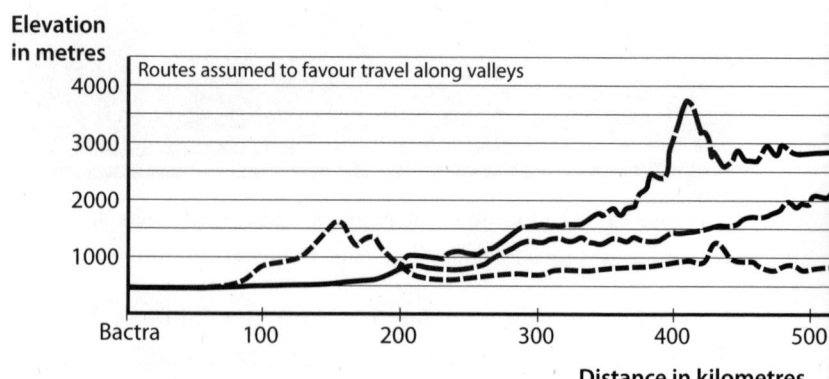

Map 6. Maes's Caravan: showing distances and elevation for main route options

A New Approach

Despite this, Falk goes on to point out a further issue regarding safety for travellers, that ought to be considered:

> There is a second reason for not using the Alai route. A number of sources say that on the upper Alai robbers posed a threat to the safety of caravans. The *Hanshu* tells us that some of the Sakas displaced by the Yuezhi lived in the mountains behind Kashgar.

The northern Ferghana Valley route would have avoided much of this heavy snowfall but not the robbers, whom Falk locates towards the border near Kashgar, whereas his preferred route by way of Tashkurgan was protected by one of the five *yabghus*, as his study of the Yuezhi highlighted. However, historian Jeffrey Lerner challenges Falk's southern route as a safe passageway:

> [We] know that during the first two centuries AD the Pamir region was in a constant state of turmoil between the numerous nomadic groups and the Chinese, who fought for control of the region south of the Pamirs where the majority of cities and trade routes were located . . . Compared to the south, the

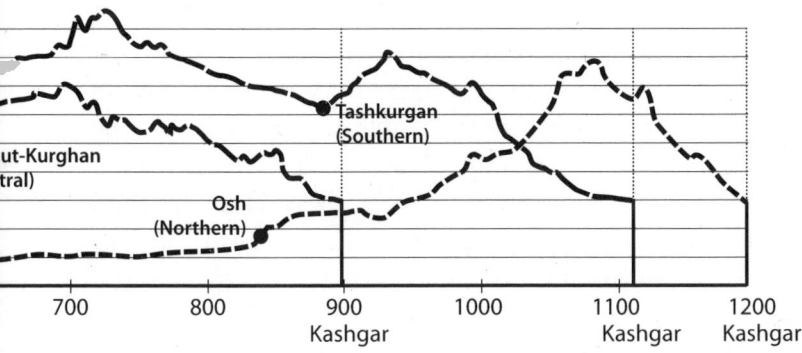

Based on Map 5, the *area* under each track is also an indicator of its degree of difficulty.

north was relatively secure, as it was under the protection of the region's greatest powers—the Chinese and the Kushans.

Lerner makes an important point here: General Ban Chao had made peace with the Kushans around AD 73 after defeating them in Kashgar, and this city then stayed in Chinese hands for over five decades. Moreover, Lerner points out that by the end of the first century, Han conquests had extended their reach to Samarkand and beyond, when they 'controlled much of Central Asia up to the Caspian'. Whether they reached all the way to this inland sea is debatable; but either way it is difficult to imagine the Protector General tolerating robbers operating near Kashgar and threatening a vital border crossing, or any Chinese trade link to the Tarim for that matter. Conversely, the Han's control of this region would have greatly added to the safety of both the northern and central routes. In suggesting that Maes's caravan chose either one of these from Bactria, Lerner adds that 'the shorter and more direct routes to Kashgar in the south were still too volatile as hostilities involving the Chinese, Kushans and "indigenous populations" had yet to be settled'. In contrast, the route through Sogdiana would have been safer considering the Sogdians maintained strong alliances with (or possibly were even a part of) both the Kushan Empire and the state of Kangju through most of this period.

There was, in fact, another route from Bactria available to Maes which other researchers have not considered. Yet it *reconciles* the northern and central routes beyond Karategin, such that his caravan need not have proceeded through the difficult Alai Valley during its final stage before arriving at the Chinese border. Stein noted this 'connector' coming the other way from Kashgar during his third expedition when, a short distance past Daraut-Kurghan, he came across: 'the entrance to the picturesque defile leading from the Alai Valley to the Tengiz-bai Pass, over which lies a direct and much-frequented route to Margilan and the rest of Ferghana'. History records the town of Margilan as having existed since at least the second century BC; later to be known as an area of silk production, and in modern times the silk capital of the USSR. This suggests that even if Stein, Bernard, and others were right in thinking that Maes's caravan took the central route after leaving Bactria, there is no reason why it could not have travelled as far as Daraut-Kurghan before turning north into the Ferghana Valley and reaching Osh via Stein's *much-frequented* Tengiz-bai Pass. (In fact, Middleton and Thomas note there is even a second connector, the Karamyk Pass, which also leads onto Osh from Daraut-Kurghan.) Thus, our third criterion, if not favouring the northern route outright, certainly makes a strong case for its use.

While the first three criteria help narrow down potential sites, our *fourth* and final criterion is the critical one. Surprisingly, though, it seems to have been overlooked by most researchers: the Stone Tower was, more than likely, established in an area capable of supporting the needs of significant amounts of caravan traffic in terms of water and pasturage for the animals, food and shelter for the accompanying travellers, and as a trading settlement for their merchandise.

We have established previously that embassies setting out from the Han capital, eager to engage with newly found nations to its west, were elaborate affairs. The caravans which made this contact possible comprised hundreds, if not thousands, of people and animals. Other than obtaining food and fodder at major stops, pack animals were often exchanged for fresh ones. Specialist animals were also engaged depending on the road ahead: camels were best in the deserts; horses or mules in the Pamir uplands; and yaks for crossing the mountain passes, since they were adept at forcing a pathway through deep snow.

We also know that the Han caravans transported enormous amounts of material (mostly merchandise) and took to the road many times a year. After skirting the Taklamakan and crossing the border, their first *lengthy* halt to recuperate and trade would, almost certainly, have been at a major settlement. And when merchants began travelling in the opposite direction, reciprocating contact with

China, their needs on arriving at the Stone Tower would have been no different.

The best indication of an area's capacity to support such an influx of caravans during this era was its population, and fortunately for us this data is available within the *Hanshu*. Its chapter on the Western Regions details the number of inhabitants who were residing at each of the four possible sites: Tashkent–600,000; Osh–300,000; Tashkurgan–5,000; and Daraut-Kurghan–1,030.* From this data it is hard to imagine how either Tashkurgan or Daraut-Kurghan could have been viable halting places capable of hosting large caravans, whereas the numbers strongly favour Tashkent and Osh. Both cities were large enough to support the multiple caravanserais needed around the Stone Tower—although being a poor match with regards to our first three criteria probably rules out Tashkent altogether. Later, as trade continued to develop, the warehouses in Osh would have allowed goods to be bought, stored, and finally sold at the opportune time.

Nestled in the Ferghana Valley, Osh has always been a veritable 'food basket' for the whole region—its very name in modern Uzbek means *pilaf* (a popular rice dish). The valley owes its fertility to two rivers, the Naryn and the Kara Darya, which unite here to form the Syr Darya (Jaxartes). Amongst its numerous other tributaries is the Ak-Buura (White Camel) River flowing just 500 metres from Sulaiman-Too. It would have offered immediate access to water for the pack animals; while the excellent pasturage in this valley is well-documented in history, including its sought-after alfalfa grass.

In summary then, of the four possible sites suggested by scholars as likely contenders for Ptolemy's famed landmark, after applying new criteria to our riddle, the one that consistently meets *every* criterion is Sulaiman-Too. Not only is it an imposing landmark

---

*   In the *Hanshu*, as noted by Hulsewe, Tashkent is taken as the state of Kangju, Osh as Da Yuan, Tashkurgan as Pu-li, and Daraut-Kurghan as Hsiu-hsun.

close to the Chinese border but, as a halting place, Osh was large enough then to satisfy the needs of the many caravans traversing the Silk Road. They stopped here to rest and trade, before continuing their journey in either direction using the relatively safe and low-cost *northern* route along the Ferghana Valley.

Compelling as they are in making the case for Sulaiman-Too, even beyond these four criteria there are other good reasons to believe that this mountain is the elusive Stone Tower, as we shall discover in the next and final chapter.

16

Solomon's Throne

To visit Sulaiman-Too and the Osh *oblast* (region) of Kyrgyzstan is a memorable experience. The melting snows from the encircling mountains feed many rivers and streams, which run down into the lush valley and give it a natural beauty that is exceptional. Its main bazaar is one of the most vibrant in Central Asia and has occupied the same site for 2,000 years. Straddling the Ak-Buura River, the bazaar stretches for a kilometre along its banks. On market days, it teems with the three main ethnic groups—Kyrgyz, Uzbeks and Tajiks—who live within this seemingly crazy patchwork of national borders created during the Soviet era. The city itself is an ancient one and intimately associated with the Silk Road from inception; it was thriving when Zhang Qian first made his way into the Ferghana Valley.

In the year 2000, Osh celebrated its 3,000th anniversary, making it the oldest city in Central Asia and older than Rome by more than two centuries. Whether Osh is precisely this age is a moot point, but the many petroglyphs which adorn the rocks on Sulaiman-Too speak to an age-old settlement. One legend suggests that it was founded by Alexander the Great as he swept through the heart of Asia. Another tells of the biblical King Solomon—also an important prophet to Muslims—placing a throne on the mountain, or perhaps building a house of worship there. A related story describes how his marching army included carriages pulled by oxen. When they reached the mountain, in calling for a halt, he shouted *Ho-Osh* (meaning 'enough'), thus giving name to the settlement and its mountain, and in the process becoming the city's patron saint of sorts. He is even supposed to have died here, and his body carried back to his native land on the back of a white camel.

On a more scientific level, Zadneprovskij has undertaken extensive excavations in and around Osh over a thirty-year period. Other local archaeologists, including Bakyt Amanbaeva, have also carried out much work in this area over many years (their findings usually published in Russian). On the mountain itself, Zadneprovskij unearthed the remains of a settlement, part of the so-called Chust culture, including mud huts, painted ceramics, utensils and graves. Radiocarbon dating has shown this settlement as being inhabited around 1000 BC. To coincide with the city reaching its three-millennia milestone, key elements of these findings were detailed in his short book *The Osh Settlement: On the History of Ferghana in the Late Bronze Age*.

The mountain, which remains the national property of the Kyrgyz Republic and is protected by law, gives the city of Osh a special character; and everywhere a visitor goes, its peaks are visible and provide a ready landmark to take one's bearings from. Many millions of years ago, it was formed through tectonic forces as the Indian plate pushed up against the Asian continent, and Sulaiman-Too continues to rise today on average by six millimetres every year. It comprises five crystal limestone hills, all stretching past 1,100 metres above sea level and each with its own name—the tallest is known as Rusha-Too (meaning 'highest' or 'brightest' mountain). Over a dozen varieties of birds make these rocky peaks their home and many others stop by during their annual migration.

Towards the back of the caravan, Kang could see a Buddhist monk fussing with his disciple and their donkey as everyone prepared to get underway at first light. The hardy pair had already crossed the dangerous mountain passes out of India—another reason for the respect accorded them by their fellow travellers—while the books they had carried back, they guarded with their lives. As far as Kang was concerned, any holy man was always welcome to join his caravan and he never charged them even a coin. He looked forward to listening to their scriptures later, seated by the campfire when the night was still and quiet. Although Kang held true to the teachings of Zoroaster and the old beliefs that had been passed down from his elders, there would be no harm in seeking blessing at the holy mountain when his caravan stood in its shadows once again. But even as he could make out its familiar outline in the distance, a mysterious illness struck him down less than a day's march from Osh and by nightfall he was gone. His sons, in stunned silence, completed what funerary rites they could the next day with help from a local priest. In keeping with their custom, they left Kang's body on one of the peaks for carrion birds to devour. Then the caravan moved on.

Beyond our four criteria, *three other reasons* support the assertion that Sulaiman-Too is Ptolemy's lost landmark. The *first* of these involve the traders who were active around the Stone Tower when it was originally established. The chronology here is important, as the kingdoms of this area and the unfolding historical events certainly would have played a major role in determining its placement.

It is generally accepted that Maes's caravan arrived at the Stone Tower around AD 100, after which he passed his report to Marinus, for Ptolemy to use some forty years later. If one assumes that at least several decades would have elapsed after the site was initially chosen as a caravan stop and before it became a well-known and frequented landmark, then this suggests the Stone Tower was founded no later than approximately AD 50. At the other end of this time frame, we know the Silk Road was initiated from the Chinese side when Han caravans started venturing out, soon after Zhang Qian's return from his first expedition in 126 BC. Within decades a route was well established, as the *Shiji* records:

> By this time, however, so many envoys had journeyed to Bactria by the northern route [around the Tarim] out of Chiu-chuan [a commandery] that the foreign states in the area had become

surfeited with Han goods and no longer regarded them with any esteem.

Clearly, the location of any major halting place would have been heavily influenced by these early caravans. Although significant maritime trade was also occurring, as far as the Stone Tower was concerned, Benjamin writes that 'the bulk of Chinese exports during the First Silk Roads Era was still travelling overland from Chang'an to Bactria'. Likewise, at the start of this era, Vaissière notes: 'The Chinese embassies, together with enormous quantities of silk, crisscrossed the area, particularly at the end of the second century BC.'*

Important, too, were the people who received these embassies on the other side—the Kushans and Sogdians. They were the middlemen whom the Han caravans dealt with after crossing over from the Tarim, with the Kushans initially leading and the Sogdians as their apprentices. Together, they controlled trade in the Ferghana Valley and Kangju. Of the Sogdians, Vaissière points out that since they 'were splendidly situated on the route from Da Yuan [Ferghana] to An-hsi† [Parthia] . . . There is no reason to suppose that they were excluded from these exchanges.' And, as we previously learnt from the *Shiji*, ambassadors from Kangju were travelling in the other direction too, presenting themselves in the Chinese capital in the final decades BC; Sima Qian described them as 'skilful at commerce and will haggle over a fraction of a cent'.

Ancient Osh was the gateway city into and out of China, lying in the midst of expert traders—when trade was the primary motivator for the Silk Road flourishing. It would have been an obvious location for a major caravan stop, and it is not difficult to envisage how the mountain that dominated it soon evolved into the Stone Tower.

---

*   Han silk fabrics dating from second century BC onwards have been excavated at the Kara-Bulak burial ground, 20 km west of Osh in the Ferghana Valley.
†   Also written as Anxi, but not to be confused with the Silk Road city near Dunhuang.

The Ferghana Valley in which Osh lies was the *second* reason for Sulaiman-Too becoming a prime destination. It was here that the Heavenly Horses were to be found which Emperor Wu had so desperately sought to assist his passage into the afterlife. For his military, the best equine bloodline was also to be found here, from which they bred the cavalry mounts needed in their life-and-death struggle against the Xiongnu. The War of the Heavenly Horses he initiated had besieged the city of Erh-shih which lay in the Ferghana Valley.* Alfalfa grass, essential for rearing these special horses, grew in abundance here, and the valley's ideal breeding conditions could not be matched in China. In fact, this valley has been home to these steeds for millennia, as the petroglyphs depicting fine-looking horses on Sulaiman-Too and the surrounding area attest to. Zadneprovskij, too, has noted 'the striking similarity of the type of Ferghana horse petroglyphs to images on Chinese tiles dating back to the last centuries BC'.

Our *third* and final reason supporting the case for Sulaiman-Too is a spiritual one—and one which has not been given due consideration by other researchers. This mountain has always held a strong religious and cultural significance for the people of this region. So much so that this was the principal reason for its being listed as a World Heritage Site by UNESCO in 2009; the citation reading: 'The site is believed to represent the most complete example of a sacred mountain anywhere in Central Asia, worshipped over several millennia.' It is reasonable, therefore, to suggest this was a sought-after location by all manner of travellers on the Silk Road. Here was a place for them to pray and seek good fortune while undertaking difficult and dangerous enterprises—akin to the Caves of the Thousand Buddhas in Dunhuang by the Jade Gate.

---

* Archaeologist Aleksandr Bernstam places Erh-shih near the ruins of Markhamat, 40 km west of Osh; while others locate it further down the valley.

Figure 14. Petroglyph of Heavenly Horse in Ferghana Valley

Figure 15. UN Postage Stamp of Sulaiman-Too

Figure 16. Kushan kings seen emerging from rock on their coins

Figure 17. Pilgrim trail on Sulaiman-Too

Figure 18. Ground gutters (left) and cup hollows (right) along trail

In fact, there is evidence of worship occurring on Sulaiman-Too even before Ptolemy's time. When Zadneprovskij excavated on this mountain, the settlement he unearthed was laid out in a step-like fashion, fifteen terraces in total covering over two hectares. Yet it was an unusual site for Chust culture because it had been built on a mountaintop; and although this feature would have made it more defendable, archaeologists do not see it as a fort. Rather, they suggest it may have been used as dwelling by a community of cult attendants who performed ritual ceremonies. It is thought to be the only such sacred mountain in this region and long sought out, even today, for its supposed ability to heal various ailments and bestow on worshippers the blessing of longevity. Women still visit Sulaiman-Too in large numbers hoping to improve their fertility, while couples wishing for a baby may stay overnight in one of the caves. Also, women having difficulty conceiving slide down over its ritual stones, while others crawl on their stomachs along the floor of the caves, in the belief that this will cure their barrenness. One other regular group of visitors to the mountain are modern-day shamans and their apprentices; yet whose rites are, somewhat surprisingly, strongly influenced by Islamic beliefs.

Possibly the earliest cult practised here, way back in time, may have been Mithraism, which originated from Persia and spread outwards both east and west including, as has been well-documented, amongst the Roman legions as the Mysteries of Mithras. (The whole subject of early religious practices propagated by migrating tribes, however, is a complex one and still not well-understood.) During their move into Central Asia, one of the Saka tribal confederations, the Haumavarga (meaning 'haoma preparers') had settled in the Ferghana Valley where they adopted a sedentary lifestyle. The Kushans, too, were associated with this Hauma cult, involving their sacred plant *haoma* and the intoxicating and hallucinogenic beverage made from it.

Some Saka venerated Mithra, with whom they associated various forms of fire and horse worship; while in Vedic texts the Indian form of this deity appears as the god of contract and mutual obligation, who was also called the Mediator. Mithraism evolved into something of a 'mystery religion' in some places, where participation was reserved to those initiated following a rite of passage, including within the ranks of battle-hardened Roman soldiers. Other rituals included the libation or pouring of haoma—a practice that links with the ground gutters and cup hollows found in and around the many caves and grottoes on Sulaiman-Too. These hollows, gouged into the stone and measuring up to twenty centimetres in diameter, are the most numerous special features observed on this mountain. Together with the long, polished gutters, which are inclined and range from 3.5 to 4.5 metres, they may have been used in rituals to imitate the well-known myth of Mithra's birth from rock inside a cave. Similar imagery is depicted on early Kushan coins, showing some of their kings, including Kanishka, emerging from rocks.

From the Chinese side also, there is some evidence in both the *Shiji* and *Hanshu* suggesting the religious importance of Sulaiman-Too (the *Shiji* represents the earliest written record of this mountain). In these texts, the capital of Ferghana was named Guishan (or Guishan-Chen), which translates as 'a town near a highly respected or sacred mountain'.

Many centuries later, as Islam began to take hold in Central Asia, Sulaiman-Too became an important pilgrimage site—legend has it that the Prophet Muhammed once prayed here, although this is doubtful. But history has recorded that around AD 1500, after inheriting the crown of Ferghana, the founder of India's Mughal Dynasty, Babur, built himself a house of worship on its slopes. In more recent times, one of the larger caves on the mountain has been turned into a small museum to house cultural artefacts and archaeological finds.

Even throughout the Soviet communist era, Sulaiman-Too managed to retain its special place with Muslims of the region. Today it is the holiest mountain in Kyrgyzstan and there are mosques and other pilgrimage stops located on a trail that runs along its slopes—many even worship here first, before beginning their Hajj to Mecca. But long before the coming of Islam, every day for millennia perhaps, the faithful have visited the mountain.

Epilogue

Recently, in an article reviewing new evidence uncovered about early Indian Buddhism, authors Salomon and Marino ended by reminding us that '[L]ack of corroboration does not prove that a statement or claim is false, but only that it is unproven. Sometimes, corroboration comes when least expected, so the door should always be left open.' Their words could just as well apply in our case.

This book has demonstrated that neither Ptolemy's data nor description are sufficient to lead us to his midpoint on the Silk Road. But by building on the work of previous scholars, before applying our four criteria and overlaying the result with three additional reasons, we may get there yet. Even taken on their own, without the 'confusion' in *Geographia*, these seven points make a compelling case for Sulaiman-Too. Of course, we will not know definitively—not until further evidence, such as new documents or other archaeological discoveries, come to light.*

Corroboration is sometimes only a chance discovery away; as Aurel Stein found when he stumbled on the Ancient Letters, and again after gaining entry to the Hidden Library in the Caves of the Thousand Buddhas. Archaeologists today readily accept that his and other expeditions in Central Asia have but scratched its surface. And

---

* In the *Handbook of Ancient Afro-Eurasian Economies* (Vol. 3) published in 2023, the editor Professor Sitta von Reden discusses Ptolemy's lost Stone Tower and agrees that it lies in Osh (Ch. 1, p. 20).

those excavating in the Tarim Basin speak of other sites lying so deep in the desert they will require helicopters to ferry in personnel and supplies, and of the need for satellite GPS (global positioning system) to locate ground crews there in the sea of shifting sand.

How many other towns and settlements lie buried in remote or inaccessible places such as the Taklamakan Desert? And what other secrets have yet to be revealed—even on the mountain itself? When proof of the location of Ptolemy's lost Stone Tower finally comes to hand, it may reveal yet another reason for the World Heritage status of Sulaiman-Too.

* * *

I have been asked how my interest was sparked in attempting to find the Stone Tower:

In 2005, I retraced the Silk Road from Istanbul to Xi'an on my own and using whatever transport was available on the day; with one change of clothes and a guidebook stuffed into a small backpack.

Travelling on a passport from a little-known nation (Fiji) had its challenges, especially securing visas for countries within Central Asia, while a few simply proved impossible. Upon arriving in Osh, I was stranded there for a week as I desperately sought a permit to enter Tajikistan and travel across the Roof of the World along the Pamir Highway (really an unsealed and treacherous road then, even in an ex-Soviet Army jeep). Later, while researching Ptolemy's Stone Tower, I realized that my time in that ancient city was probably spent in the shadows of his famous landmark.

Acknowledgements

There are a number of people in various countries whose assistance and support I gratefully acknowledge as this book grew from an idea into reality—although any errors in it are entirely mine.

Foremost is Professor Emeritus Daniel Waugh, long-time editor of *The Silk Road* based in Seattle, whose help and advice led to my article being published in that journal, without which this book would not have followed. When it finally did, leading up to its initial publication in 2022, during the process I received invaluable assistance from my editors at Penguin Random House (India), Manasi Subramaniam, Binita Roy and Shubhi Surana, manuscript assessor Anushree Kaushal, and agent Anish Chandy of Labyrinth Literary Agency, all based in Delhi. My thanks to Dr Michael Pearson of Canberra for also reviewing the manuscript. And for this second publication by Casemate (UK), I am grateful to publisher Ruth Sheppard and editor Isobel Fulton for their assistance.

The maps in this book, as in my previous one, were produced by Roger Smith of Geographx in Wellington (despite his protests of having retired this time around). Also from New Zealand are a friend and a chance acquaintance, both of whom assisted with language translations: Paul Fitzgerald with French, and Zena Lichtwark with Russian. Gordon Lee from England prepared the final image demonstrating Eratosthenes's method. My fragmented story about Kang's family of caravanners was inspired by Dr Susan Whitfield's

Life Along the Silk Road and her sound advice over a coffee in London to 'just write about the things that interest you'. Dr Bakyt Amanbaeva kindly secured permission from her government in Kyrgyzstan for use of their images of *the* mountain I was confronted with upon arriving in Osh.

While backpacking the old Silk Road, I managed to travel through much of Central Asia by utilizing the services of David Berghof of Stan Tours operating out of Kazakhstan. Finally, I was only able to make this once-in-a-lifetime journey thanks to my wife Beth, who unselfishly stayed at home (at the time in Sydney) with our three sons—for good reason, this book is dedicated to her.

Appendix

Three more translations from *Geographia* (Book I, Chapter 12) are shown below,* describing the route taken by the caravan of Maes Titianus from Bactria to the Stone Tower:

(i) Henry Yule (1866)
Thence the road proceeds eastward to Bactra, and from that northward up the ascent of the hill country of the Komedai, and then inclining somewhat south through the hill country itself as far as the gorge in which the plains terminate. For the *western* end of the hill country is more to the *north* also, being (as Marinus puts it) under the latitude of Byzantium, the *eastern* end more to the *south* being under the latitude of Hellespont. Hence [the hills running thus from south of east to north of west] the road runs as he describes in the opposite direction, *i.e.* towards the east with an inclination south; and then a distance of fifty schoinoi extending to the Stone Tower would seem to tend northward. This Stone Tower stands in the way of those who ascend the gorge, and from it the mountains extend eastward to join the chain of Imaon which runs north to this from (the territory of) Palimbothra.

---

* Place names have been standardized so as not to unduly confuse readers.

(ii) J. W. McCrindle (1883)

The route after this runs in an eastward direction to Bactria whence it turns towards the north in ascending the mountains of the Komedai, and then in passing through these mountains it pursues a southern course as far as the ravine that opens into the plain country. For the northern parts of the mountain region and those furthest to the west where the ascent begins, are placed by him under the parallel of Byzantium, and those in the south and the east under the parallel of the Hellespont. For this reason, he says, that this route makes a detour of equal length in opposite directions, that in advancing to the east it bends towards the south, and thereafter probably runs up towards the north for fifty schoinoi, till it reaches the Stone Tower. For to quote his own words, 'When the traveller has ascended the ravine he arrives at the Stone Tower, after which the mountains that trend to the east unite with Imaon, the range that runs up to the north from Palimbothra.'

(iii) Edward Luther Stevenson (1932)

From Antioch to Bactria the journey deviates to the east, and after ascending the Komedai mountains it bends to the north. From the mountains, where it comes to the plain at their base, it inclines to the south, for the mountains extend north and east. The ascent is placed by Marinus on the Byzantium parallel, and the southern and eastern ranges are located on the Hellespont parallel. The mountains themselves he places east, but plainly extends them so as partially to decline to the south. Likewise he says that the journey for fifty schoinoi before coming to the Stone Tower, deviates to the north. When you have traversed the plain, at the base to the mountains you arrive at the Stone Tower, and from there you come to the mountains which run in an easterly direction, ending at Imaon which is north of Palimbothra.

Image Credits

Figure 1. Dunhuang Academy; image of mural in Mogao Cave 323
Figure 2. Photo by author taken in 2005 at Jade Gate
Figure 3. From Wikimedia Commons; photo by G41rn8 at Gansu Provincial Museum
Figures 4 and 16. CNG (www.cngcoins.com)
Figure 5. Inset photo by J. Thomson, The Grosvenor Studios, 1909; main photo by Aurel Stein
Figures 6, 7, 8 and 9. From *On Ancient Central-Asian Tracks*, Figures 31, 74, 86 and 92 respectively
Figure 10. From Wikimedia Commons; final image by C.M.G. Lee
Figure 11. From *Facsimile-Atlas to the Early History of Cartography*, Map XXII (top); and University of Alabama Map Library, image by Thomas Porcacchi, via Wikimedia Commons (bottom)
Figures 12, 14, 17 and 18. From *Nomination of Sulaiman-Too Cultural Landscape*, Supplement V photos numbered 3 and 92, 115, 40, 34 and 25 respectively
Figure 13. NASA's Earth Observatory; image by Jeff Schmaltz
Figure 15. United Nations Postal Administration

While every effort has been made to secure permissions for images and quotations, the author regrets any inadvertent omission in failing to trace a copyright holder.

Timeline of Key Events

BC	West of the Stone Tower	BC	East of the Stone Tower
c. 250	Parthian Empire established; Greco-Bactrian Kingdom emerges	221	Qin Dynasty begins—ends 207 BC
		209	Modu becomes shanyu of Xiongnu
		206	Former Han Dynasty begins—ends AD 9
		c. 173	Yuezhi attack Wusun, who flee to Xiongnu
		162	Xiongnu defeat Yuezhi in Gansu; Yuezhi oust Saka to occupy Ili Valley
c. 140	Northern Bactria overrun by Saka	141	Emperor Wu starts reign of 54 years
		139	Zhang Qian starts journey west
		132	Wusun eject Yuezhi from Ili Valley
130	Yuezhi settle on northern bank of Oxus	c. 131	Yuezhi pass through Ferghana
128	Zhang Qian reaches Yuezhi		
c. 125	Greco-Bactrian Kingdom ends	126	Zhang Qian returns from first expedition
		119	Zhang Qian visits Wusun
		101	Heavenly Horses from Ferghana arrive in China

BC	West of the Stone Tower	BC	East of the Stone Tower
		c. 100	First Silk Roads Era begins
c. 80	Yuezhi cross Oxus into Bactria proper	94	*Shiji* completed by Sima Qian
c. 30	Sogdian long-range trade begins	59	Western Regions established by Han
27	Roman Empire established		
AD		AD	
25	Kushan Empire begins	25	Later Han Dynasty begins
100	Caravan of Maes Titianus at Stone Tower	91	Ban Chao installed as Protector General
140	*Geographia* written by Claudius Ptolemy	121	*Hanshu* completed by Ban Biao

> 220–225 Han Dynasty, Kushan and Parthian empires all come to an end.
> c. 250 First Silk Roads Era ends.

Glossary

An-hsi	ancient Chinese name for Parthia
Anxi	Chinese Silk Road city near Dunhuang
Bactria	classical Greek kingdom (northern Afghanistan)
Byzantium	original name for Constantinople (later Istanbul)
Chang'an	initial capital of Han Dynasty (present-day Xi'an)
Da Yuan	early Chinese name for Ferghana
Erh-shih	ancient capital of Ferghana (near Samarkand)
Geographia	text by Claudius Ptolemy (completed c. AD 140)
guan	Chinese frontier pass
heqin	peace and affinity (in Chinese)
Hanshu	or *Book of Han* by Ban Gu (completed c. AD 112)
haoma	sacred plant, as well as the drink made from it
Hellespont	Dardanelles waterway separating Europe and Asia
hormeterion	trading post or base
Hou Hanshu	or *Book of Later Han* by Fan Ye (completed fifth century AD)
Imaon	parts of Pamirs, Tien Shan and Himalayas

Kangju	ancient state which probably included Sogdiana
Karategin	region in southern Tajikistan along Vakhsh River
Kharosthi	early Indian alphabetic script
Komedai	refers to the Saka tribes (as used by Ptolemy)
li	approx. 400 metres (ancient Chinese measurement)
limes	series of defensive watchtowers, walls and forts
Lithinos Pyrgos	Stone Tower in romanized Greek
Loulan	ancient Chinese kingdom by Lop Nor
Luoyang	later capital of Han Dynasty (still a major city)
oikoumene	the known or inhabited world
Palimbothra	ancient Indian city (near present-day Patna)
pamir	valley plain surrounded by high mountains
Parthia	ancient Persia/Iran
podboy	tomb built as an underground chamber
Saka	nomadic tribes of northern Asia (also known as Shaka, Scythian or Sai)
satrapy	province ruled by a governor in ancient Persia
schoinoi	equal to 30 stades (Greco-Roman measurement)
Seres	classical Greco-Roman name for China
shanyu	supreme leader of the Xiongnu
Shentu	early Chinese name for India
Shiji	or *Records of the Grand Historian* by Sima Qian (completed c. 94 BC)
Shu	country in ancient China (present-day Sichuan)
stade	approx. 158 metres (Greco-Roman measurement)

stupa	mound-like Buddhist funeral structure
sutra	sermon of the historical Buddha
Tianzhu	early Chinese name for Northwest India
too	mountain (in Kyrgyz)
Turris Lapidea	Stone Tower in Latin
Wusun	tribe neighbouring the Xiongnu and Yuezhi
Xiongnu	nomadic empire rivalling Han Dynasty
yabghu	prince of a tribal division of the Yuezhi
Yuezhi	nomadic tribe of the Western Regions who eventually migrated to northern India
yurt	traditional tent dwelling made of felt

Select Bibliography

Andrade, Nathanael. 2015. 'The Voyage of Maes Titianos and the Dynamics of Social Connectivity between the Roman Levant and Central Asia/West China'. *Mediterraneo Antico*, 41–74.
Andrea, Alfred. 2014. 'The Silk Road in World History: A Review Essay'. *Asian Review of World Histories*, 105–127.
Benjamin, Craig. 2007. *The Yuezhi*. Turnhout, Belgium: Brepolis Publishers.
———. 2018. *Empires of Ancient Eurasia*. Cambridge: Cambridge University Press.
Berggren, J. Lennart, and Alexander Jones. 2000. *Ptolemy's Geography: An Annotated Translation of the Theoretical Chapters*. Princeton: Princeton University Press.
Bernard, Paul. 2005. 'De l'Euphrate a la Chine avec la caravane de Maes Titianos'. *Comptes rendus des séances de l'Academie des Inscriptions et Belles Lettres*, 929–969.
Bonavia, Judy. 1988. *The Silk Road*. London: Collins.
Boulnois, Luce. 1966. *The Silk Road* (trans. by D. Chamberlain). New York: E. P. Dutton.
———. 2004. *Silk Road: Monks, Warriors and Merchants on the Silk Road* (trans. by H. Loveday). Hong Kong: Odyssey.
Bregel, Yuri. 2003. *An Historical Atlas of Central Asia*. Leiden: Brill.
Brown, Lloyd A. 1949. *The Story of Maps*. Boston: Little Brown & Co.

Bunbury, E. H. 1883. *A History of Ancient Geography*. London: John Murray.
Carr, Geoffrey. 2005. 'The Proper Study of Mankind: A Survey of Human Evolution'. *Economist*, December 24, 3–12.
Cary, Max. 1956. 'Maes, qui et Titianus'. *The Classical Quarterly 6/3–4*, 130–134.
Cosmo, Nicola Di. 2011. 'Ethnogenesis, Coevolution and Political Morphology of the Earliest Steppe Empire: The Xiongnu Question Revisited'. In *Xiongnu Archaeology: Multidisciplinary Perspectives of the First Steppe Empire in Inner Asia*, 35–48.
Dean, Riaz. 2015. 'The Location of Ptolemy's Stone Tower: The Case for Sulaiman-Too in Osh'. *The Silk Road*, 75–83.
———. 2019. *Mapping the Great Game*. Delhi: Penguin Random House India, and Oxford: Casemate.
Falk, Harry. 2018. 'The Five Yabghus of the Yuezhi'. *Bulletin of Asia Institute (N. S., Vol. 28)*, 1–46.
Flecker, James Elroy. 1922. *Hassan: The Story of Hassan of Bagdad and How He Came to Make the Golden Journey to Samarkand* (A Play in Five Acts). London: William Heinemann.
Frankopan, Peter. 2015. *The Silk Roads: A New History of the World*. London: Bloomsbury.
Hansen, Valerie. 2012. *The Silk Road: A New History*. Oxford: Oxford University Press.
Harley, J. B., and David Woodward (eds). 1987. *History of Cartography* (Vol. 1). Chicago: University of Chicago Press.
Harmatta, Janos (ed.). 1994. *History of Civilisations of Central Asia* (Vol. II). Paris: UNESCO Publishing.
Hill, John. 2009. *Through the Jade Gate to Rome*. Author.
Hopkirk, Peter. 1980. *Foreign Devils on the Silk Road*. London: John Murray.
Hulsewe, A. F. P. and M. A. N. Loewe. 1979. *China in Central Asia, the Early Stage: 125 BC–AD 23*. Leiden: Brill.

Juping, Yang. 2013. 'The Relations between China and India and the Opening of the Southern Silk Road During the Han Dynasty'. *The Silk Road,* 82–92.

Lerner, Jeffrey. 1998. 'Ptolemy and the Silk Road: From Baktra Basileion to Sera Metropolis'. *East and West,* 9–25.

Lindesay, William. 2015. *The Great Wall in 50 Objects.* Beijing: Penguin Random House China.

Liu, Xinru. 2010. *The Silk Road in World History.* Oxford: Oxford University Press.

Man, John. 2019. *Barbarians at the Wall.* London: Bantam Press.

McCrindle, J. M. 1885. *Ancient India as Described by Ptolemy.* London: Trubner & Co.

Michaud, Roland and Sabina. 1978. *Caravans to Tartary.* London: Thames and Hudson.

Middleton, Robert, and Huw Thomas. 2008. *Tajikistan and the High Pamirs: A Companion and Guide.* Hong Kong: Odyssey Books & Guides.

Miller, Innes J. 1969. *The Spice Trade of the Roman Empire.* Oxford: Clarendon Press.

Millward, James. 2013. *The Silk Road: A Very Short Introduction.* Oxford: Oxford University Press.

Mirsky, Jeannette. 1977. *Sir Aurel Stein: Archaeological Explorer.* Chicago: University of Chicago Press.

Morgan, Gerald. 1973. 'The Heavenly Horses'. *History Today,* February, 77–83.

Narain, A. K. 1957. *The Indo-Greeks.* Oxford: Clarendon Press.

———. 1997–98. 'The Coins and Identity of the Nameless Yuezhi King of Bactria', *Asia Institute Torino,* 561–579.

Neelis, Jason. 2007. 'Passages to India: Saka and Kusana Migrations in Historical Contexts'. In *On the Cusp of an Era: Art in the Pre-Kusana World,* by Doris Srinivassan, 55–93. Leiden: Brill.

Nordenskiold, A. E. 1889. *Facsimile-Atlas to the Early History of Cartography* (trans. by J. Ekelof and C. Markham). Stockholm (repr. 1973. New York: Dover Publications).

P'iankov, Igor'. 2015. 'Maes Titianus, Ptolemy, and the "Stone Tower" on the Great Silk Road'. *The Silk Road*, 60–74.

Rapin, Claude. 2001. 'L'incompréhensible Asie central de la carte de Ptolémée. Propositions pour un décodage.' *Bulletin of the Asia Institute (N. S., Vol. 12)*, 201–225.

Rawlinson, Henry. 1872. 'Monograph on the Oxus'. *The Journal of the Royal Geographic Society (Vol. 42)*, 482–513.

Rolfe, John (trans.). 1940. *Ammianus Marcellinus* (Vol. II). Cambridge: Harvard University Press.

Salomon, Richard, and Joseph Marino. 2014. *Observations on the Deorkothar Inscriptions and Their Significance for the Evaluation of Buddhist Historical Traditions*. Tokyo: ARIRIAB (Vol. XVII).

'Silk Road Exhibit'. https://depts.washington.edu/silkroad/exhibit/index2.html.

'Silk Road Foundation'. http://www.silkroadfoundation.org/toc/index.html.

'Silk Road Seattle'. https://depts.washington.edu/silkroad/index.html.

Sima Qian: *see* Watson, Burton.

Sims-Williams, Nicholas. 2004. *The Sogdian Ancient Letters: 1, 2, 3 and 5*. https://depts.washington.edu/silkroad/texts/sogdlet.html.

———. 2012. 'Bactrian Historical Inscriptions of the Kushan Period'. *The Silk Road*, 76–80.

Stein, Aurel. 1900. *Kalhana's Rajatarangini*. Westminster: Constable.

———. 1903. *Sand Buried Ruins of Khotan*. London: T. Fisher Unwin.

———. 1907. *Ancient Khotan*. Oxford: Clarendon Press.

———. 1921. *Serindia*. Oxford: Clarendon Press.

———. 1928. *Innermost Asia*. Oxford: Clarendon Press.

———. 1933. *On Ancient Central-Asian Tracks*. London: Macmillan.

Stevenson, Edward Luther (trans.). 1932. *Geography of Claudius Ptolemy*. New York: The New York Public Library.

Strathern, Paul. 1993. *Silk and Spice Routes: Land*. London: UNESCO.

'Sulaiman-Too Sacred Mountain'. https://whc.unesco.org/en/list/1230/documents/.
Tarn, W. W. 1938. *The Greeks in Bactria and India*. Cambridge: Cambridge University Press.
Ten Grotenhuis, Elizabeth (ed.). 2002. *Along the Silk Road*. Washington DC: Sackler Gallery.
'The International Dunhuang Project'. http://idp.bl.uk.
Thomson, J. Oliver. 1948. *History of Ancient Geography*. Cambridge: Cambridge University Press.
Tooley, R. V. 1949. *Maps and Map-Makers*. London: Batsford.
Tucker, Jonathan. 2015. *The Silk Road: Central Asia, Afghanistan and Iran*. London: I. B. Tauris.
———. 2015. *The Silk Road: China and the Karakorum Highway*. London: I. B. Tauris.
Tupikova, Irina, Matthias Schemmel, and Klaus Geus. 2014. *Travelling along the Silk Road: A New Interpretation of Ptolemy's Coordinates (Preprint 465)*. Berlin: Max Planck Institute for the History of Science.
UNESCO Nomination, The National Academy of Sciences of Kyrgyz Republic. 2005. *Nomination of Sulaiman-Too Cultural Landscape* [for UNESCO World Heritage List]. Bishkek.
Vaissière, Étienne de La. 2005. *Sogdian Traders: A History* (trans. by J. Ward). Leiden: Brill.
von Reden, Sitta. 2023. *Handbook of Ancient Afro-Eurasian Economies (Volume 3: Frontier-Zone Processes and Transimperial Exchange)*. Oldenbourg: De Gruyter.
Waley, Arthur. 1955. 'The Heavenly Horses of Ferghana: A New View'. *History Today*, February, 95–103.
———. 1960. *Ballads and Stories from Tun-huang*. London: George Allen & Unwin.
Walker, Annabel. 1995. *Aurel Stein: Pioneer of the Silk Road*. London: John Murray.
Watson, Burton. 1958. *Ssu Ma Chien Grand Historian of China*. New York: Columbia University Press.

———. (trans.) 1961. *Records of the Grand Historian of China* (2 volumes) (trans. from the *Shih chi* of Ssu-ma Chien). New York: Columbia University Press.
Whitfield, Roderick, Susan Whitfield, and Neville Agnew. 2000. *Cave Temples of Mogao*. Los Angles: The Getty Conservation Institute.
Whitfield, Susan. 1999. *Life Along the Silk Road*. London: John Murray.
———. 2004. *Aurel Stein on the Silk Road*. London: The British Museum Press.
——— (ed.). 2004. *The Silk Road: Trade, Travel, War and Faith*. London: British Library.
———. 2009. 'Stein's Silk Road Legacy Revisited'. *Asian Affairs*, 224–242.
Wilcken, Ulrich (trans. by G. Richards). 1967. *Alexander the Great*. New York: W. W. Norton.
Wood, Frances. 2002. *The Silk Road*. London: Folio Society.
Yule, Henry. 1866. *Cathay and the Way Thither*. London: Hakluyt Society.
———. 1903. *The Book of Ser Marco Polo*. New York: Charles Scribner's Sons.
Zadneprovskij, J. A. 2000. *The Osh Settlement: On the History of Ferghana in the Late Bronze Age*. Bishkek: Kyrghyz Republic National Academy of Science.

Index

Afghanistan, 25, 27, 58, 87, 94, 110, 157, 168
Africa, 58, 142, 144
Agathodaimon (Alexandrian draughtsman), 146
Ak-Buura River, 184, 186
Alai Mountains, 165
Alai Valley, 131, 162, 164–65, 167–68, 179–182
al-Biruni (Arab polymath), 170
Alexander the Great, 79–80, 97–98, 144, 164, 186, 141–42
Alexandria (city and port), 138–142, 145–46, 152
alfalfa, 24, 32, 41–42, 100, 184, 190
Ammianus Marcellinus (Vol II), 166
Amanbaeva, Bakyt, 187
Amu Darya (Oxus River), 24, 168, 184
Ancient Khotan, 152
Ancient India as Described by Ptolemy, 138
Ancient Letters, 102, 118, 195
Andrade, Nathanael, 155

Andrea, Alfred, 4
Anxi, 47, 59, 189
An-hsi (Parthia), 98, 189
Antiochus, Emperor, 98
Aornos (ancient battle site), 104
Apama (daughter of Spitamenes), 98
Arabian Sea, 152
Aryan, xiii, 88, 96
Ashoka the Great, 91
Augustus, Emperor, 58, 155

Babur, Emperor, 193
Bactra (capital of Bactria), 25, 160, 164, 179, 199
Bactria/Bactrian Empire, vi, 25, 27, 29, 39, 45, 79–83, 90, 96, 96–97, 103, 136, 152–53, 159–60, 162, 164, 168–69, 174, 176, 182–83, 188–89, 199–200
Bactrian camel, 52–53, 109, 168
Bactrian language and script, 86, 88, 93
Balkh (Bactra), 25, 80

Ballads and Stories from Tun-huang, 64
Ban Chao, 84–86, 155, 182
Ban Gu, 9
Ban Zhao, 9
barbarians, 6, 8, 11, 14, 18, 24, 27–28, 30–31, 34–35, 97, 175
Barthold, W., 81
Battuta, Ibn, 64
Bei shi (History of the Northern Dynasties), 66
Becker, Jasper, 33
Belt and Road Initiative (BRI), 69
Benjamin, Craig, xiii, 31, 35, 82, 94, 189
Berggren, J. Lennart, 145–46, 151, 161
Bernard, Paul, 166–67, 183
Bernstam, Aleksandr, 190
bodhisattvas, 91, 122
Bombyx mori (silkworm), 63
Boulnois, Luce, 61, 65, 92
Bregel, Yuri, 178
British Museum, 86, 129
Brown, Lloyd, 139
Buddha (Siddhartha Gautama), 52, 67–68, 89, 92–94, 121–22, 126–28
Buddhism
    in China, 67, 92, 101
    in India, 69, 195
    Kanishka's patronage of, 91
    Mahayana (Great Vehicle), 91
    nirvana, 92
    seven gems of, 93
    Sogdian's patronage of, 101
    spread of, 67, 111
    as state religion of China, 68
Buddhist Road, 91
Bunbury, Edward, 157–159
Byzantium (Constantinople), 146–147, 158, 160, 199–200

Campaigns of Alexander, The, 104
caravan(s)
    first caravans, 44–55
    leader, 44, 49, 54, 92, 178
    routes, xii, 84, 167
    stops, 54, 173, 178, 188–89
    trade, 51, 55, 60, 93, 99, 150
caravanners, xiii, 51, 54–55, 168, 197
caravanserais, 54–55, 57, 73, 103–4, 115, 151, 174, 184
Caravans to Tartary, 168
Carr, Geoffrey, 5
Carrhae, Battle of (53 BC), 59
cartography, 137–38, 141, 143–45, 147, 159, 170
Cary, Max, 155
Caspian Sea, 11, 76, 144, 182
Cathay and the Way Thither, 170
Caves of the Thousand Buddhas, 121, 190, 195
Chang'an, 10, 30, 45, 149, 189
Chavannes, Édouard, 102
Chinese *Limes*, 116, 121
Chinese Turkestan, 106, 112
Chust culture, 187, 192
Coates, Austin, 33
codex archetypus, 105–6
Columbus, Christopher, 138, 144
Constantinople (Istanbul), *See* Byzantium

copper currency, 75, 108, 116, 153
Cosmo, Di Nicola, 11
Cribb, Joe, 86, 88

Daraut-Kurghan, 131, 164–67, 176–78, 180, 183–84
Dark Ages, 57
Davids, Thomas and Caroline Rhys, 93
Dead Sea Scrolls, 128
Dialogues of the Buddha, 92
Diamond Sutra, 127
die Seidenstrasse. See Silk Road
Dilke, O. A. W., 144, 159
Dunhuang, 38, 40, 47, 55, 64, 74, 116, 120–21, 125, 129, 136, 167, 175, 189
Dzungaria Gate, 175

Egypt(ian), 58, 67, 138–39
Eighth Map of Asia, 169
Eratosthenes, 139–41, 144, 157–58
Erh-shih, 37–38, 40, 190
Euphrates River, 59, 154, 158
Eurasian Steppe, 11–12, 77, 175

Facsimile-Atlas to the Early History of Cartography, 170
Falk, Harry, 84, 167–169, 179, 181
Fan Ye, 83
Faxian, 52, 92
Ferghana, kingdom, 24, 26, 37, 65, 161
Ferghana Valley, 24, 79, 95–96, 162, 172, 174, 176, 178, 181, 183–186, 189–92

first caravans, 45–55
Five Yabghus of the Yuezhi, The, 169
Flecker, James Elroy, 49
Fortunate Islands (Canary Islands), 149–51
Four Great Inventions, 68–69
Frankopan, Peter, 69
Foguoji, (A Record of Buddhistic Kingdoms), 52

Gandhara, 93–94, 111
Ganfu (guide), 22, 25–26
Ganges River, 27, 82, 153
Gansu Corridor, 10–12, 39, 42, 45, 74, 100, 175
Gansu Province, 11, 46, 78
Gan Ying, 155
Gaoseng Zhuan (Biographies of Eminent Monks), 101
Gaugamela, Battle of (331 BC), 141
Geographia, vi, xi, xiii, 50, 74, 78, 90, 96, 110, 131, 135–48, 151–54, 156, 160–62, 167, 169, 172–73, 176, 195, 199
glass (including glassware), 58, 59, 66, 116
Gobi Desert, 46, 48
gold (including coins and thread), 17, 18, 29, 37, 42, 51, 60, 63, 67, 75, 88–89, 93, 115, 130
Golden Peninsula (Malaya), 153
Grand Historian, The. *See* Sima Qian
Grand Trunk Road, 94
grapes (including grapevines), 26, 65–66

Great Harbour (of Alexandria), 138
Great Library of Alexandria, 138
Great Wall of China, 8, 11–12, 16,
   19, 33, 38, 46–47, 117, 120,
   166
Greco-Bactrian Kingdom, 80,
   97–98
Greco-Roman, 57, 112, 138–140,
   152
Greek(s), 3, 11, 24–25, 62, 74, 79,
   80–81, 86, 88–89, 92, 96–97,
   103–4, 115, 135–36, 138,
   143, 145, 149, 152, 161, 167
Greeks in Bactria and India, The,
   152
Guard the Frontiers and Protect the Borders, 35
Gutenberg Bible, 127

Han army, 18, 28, 35, 38–39, 41
Han caravans, 99, 183, 188–89
Han Dynasty, 5, 9, 17, 30, 68, 83,
   131
   barbarians greedy for wealth
      and goods of, 28
   expansion of Middle
      Kingdom, 30, 42
   export of Chinese goods, 58
   golden age of, 58
   'hand of friendship' to Yuezhi,
      25
   import of Mongolian ponies,
      33
   matrimonial alliance with
      Wusun, 30
   sending envoys to newly found
      nations, 44
   struggle with Xiongnu Empire,
      19–20
   visit of Wusun ambassadors,
      30
Hansen, Valerie, 57, 65, 155
Hanshu (Book of Han), 9, 16–17,
   83, 100, 175, 181, 184, 193
haoma/Hauma (cult), 192–93
Heavenly Horses, 30, 32–43, 190
   depictions in Chinese art, 42
   hymns about, 34–35
   mountain-bred horses, 36
   rearing of, 36, 42
   stud farms, 42
   sweating blood, 41
   War of the Heavenly Horses
      (104 BC), 37–41
Hedin, Sven, 106, 116
Hellespont, 151, 158, 160,
   199–200
heqin (peace and affinity) strategy,
   15, 19
Hexi Corridor. *See* Gansu Corridor
Hidden Library, 115–31
Hierapolis, 151, 154, 166
Hill, John, 9, 67
Himalayas, 160
Hinduism, 69
Hindu Kush, 64, 77, 84
Historical Atlas of Central Asia, An,
   178
History of Ancient Geography (Vol 1), 144, 157
hormeterion, 151, 162, 165
horse(s)
   breeding in China, 33
   depictions in Chinese art, 42

of Ferghana, 37
golden, 37
Heavenly Horses (*see* Heavenly Horses)
Mongolian ponies, 36
petroglyph, 190–91
racing of, 33
rearing of, 36, 41–42
supreme weapon of war, 36
worship, 192
Hou Hanshu (Book of Later Han), 9, 67, 83–86, 91
Huang Di (semi-mythical Emperor), 3
Huang He (Yellow River), 12
Hulsewe, A. F. P., 9, 17, 29, 184
Huns, 11, 119, 166

I Ching (Book of Changes), 34
Imaon (mountain range), 50, 160, 199–200
India, vi, xi, 27, 30, 45, 47, 52, 59–60, 62, 64, 67, 69, 73, 77, 80–82, 84–85, 87–88, 91–94, 101–02, 104–105, 107–108, 111, 125, 129, 153, 169, 174, 187, 193
    gold coins of, 88
    maritime trade with Rome, 82
    Saka Era, 77
    Tianzhu (Northwest India), 67, 91, 102
    Yuezhi-Kushans migration into, 88
Indian(s), 11, 58, 62, 74, 77, 82–83, 85, 89–91, 93–94, 101, 106, 111, 113, 120–22, 127, 139, 153, 168, 187, 193, 195
Indian Buddhist artworks, 121
Indian Great Road, 94
Indian Institute Library, 106
Indian Ocean, 144, 152
Indus River, 91, 98,
Indus Valley, 80, 101, 153
Innermost Asia, 164
Integral Study of the Silk Road: Roads of Dialogue, 136
International Dunhuang Project, 127, 129, 136
Islam(ic), 120, 145, 170, 192–94

jade, 38, 47, 66 74–75
Jade Gate, 38–39, 41, 47, 62, 113, 119, 121, 190
Jaxartes River (Syr Darya), 24, 96–97, 184
Jiang Siye, 107, 117, 123, 126
Jing Di, Emperor, 35
Jizhu (shanyu), 76
Jones, Alexander, 145–46, 151, 161
Justinus (Roman writer), 80

Kadphises, Vima, 86, 88, 90
Kabul, 84, 158
Kaffirs' Castle, 86
Kang (caravanner), 73–74, 83, 95–96, 104, 115, 137, 149, 174, 187–88
Kangju, 24, 79, 85, 96, 99, 100, 102, 175, 182, 184, 189
Kanishka, King, 82, 87, 89, 90–91, 94, 193

Kara-Bulak, 189
Karakoram Highway, 101, 109, 167
Karamyk Pass, 183
Karategin (region), 162, 164–65, 168, 174, 182
Karategin-Alai Valley, 180
Kashgar, 47, 50, 55, 84, 86, 131, 167–68, 180–82
Kashmir, 77, 84, 91, 101, 105–06, 109, 113, 130
Kattigara, 153
Kharosthi (ancient script), 93–94, 124
Khotan, 38, 47, 74, 84, 88, 111–14
Khujand, 37, 97
Komedai (Saka tribes), 148, 151, 160, 164–68, 199–200
Konow, Sten, 77
Kujula Kadphises, King, 84–88, 90, 169
Kunlun Mountains, 35, 46, 74
Kunmo, 29–30, 78
Kushan Empire, 58, 68, 70, 73, 81, 82–94, 124, 169, 174
   birth of, 83
   coinage of, 87–88, 191, 193
   defeat by Ban Chao, 86
   Eastern Division of, 91
   expansion of, 85
   Great Kushans era, 82, 89
   incursion into China, 86
   conquest of Ganges Valley, 91
   Kalhana's account of, 105
   royal lineage of four kings, 87
Kushan merchants, xiii, 92

Kyrgyzstan, xiii, 24, 136, 165, 170, 186, 193, 197

Lady Li, 38
Lake Issyk-Kul, 28, 76–77
Lattimore, Owen, 164
Le Coq, Albert von, 53
Lerner, Jeffrey, 181–82
Li Guangli, General, 6, 38–41
Li Ling, General, 6
limes (fortifications), 116–17, 121
Liu, Xinru, 92–93
Lop Desert, 47, 116
Lop Nor (lake), 24, 116, 153
Loulan, 16–17, 24, 47, 85, 116, 120
Luoyang, 119, 149, 166–67

Maes (and his caravan), 130, 154–160, 163, 167–68, 172, 174, 176, 180–83, 188, 199
Mahabharata, 74, 96
Man, John, 7–8, 13
Mapping the Great Game, 157, 168
Maracanda. *See* Samarkand
Marcellinus, Ammianus, 165–66
Marco Polo, 49–50, 110, 116, 131, 164
Margilan, 182
Marinus (of Tyre), 143, 151, 154–59, 162, 165, 172, 188, 199–200
Maritime Silk Road, 47, 69, 153
Mathura, 94
Maurya Empire, 153
Max Planck Institute, 169, 172
Maximus Planudes, 146, 161

McCrindle, J. W., 138, 148, 161, 167, 170, 200
Memoir of the Ancient Geography of Kashmir, A, 106
Menander (Indo-Greek king), 92
Michaud, Roland and Sabina, 168
Middle Ages, xii, 139
Middle Kingdom, 3, 11, 42, 67–68
Middleton, Robert, 168–69, 183
Millward, James, 65
Ming, Emperor, 67
Mirsky, Jeannette, 103, 128
Mithra(ism), 67, 192–93
Modu, (shanyu), 15–17, 25, 75–76
Mogao Caves. *See* Caves of the Thousand Buddhas
Mohand Marg (Kashmir), 105–06
Mongol Empire, 68
Mongolian ponies, 33, 36
Mongols/Mongolia, 12, 14, 33
Morgan, Gerald, 33
Mughal Dynasty, 193
Murex sea snails, 61
Muslim, 146, 186, 193
Mysteries of Mithras, 192

Nanai-vandak (Sogdian trader), 101, 167
Narain, A. K., 80, 82, 90
NASA (satellite image), 178–79
National Museum of Afghanistan, 87
National Museum of India, 112, 130
Natural History, 60
New Delhi, 112, 130
Nile River and delta, 138, 140–141

Nordenskiold, A. E., 170

oasis/oases settlement(s), 46, 49, 53–55, 74, 94, 108, 111, 116, 174
oikoumene (known world), 50, 141, 143–44, 149
On Alexander's Track to the Indus, 110
On Ancient Central-Asian Tracks, 130
Ordos, 12
Osh Settlement: On the History of Ferghana in the Late Bronze Age, The, 187
Ottoman Turks, 147
Osh, 57, 170, 172, 176, 178–79, 183–190, 196, 198
Oxus River, 24–25, 79, 81–83, 85, 96, 110, 115, 164, 168

Pakistan, 94, 101
Palimbothra (Pataliputra), 153, 160, 199–200
Pamir Mountains, 50, 77, 85, 91, 130–31, 136, 160, 162, 168–69, 175, 179–181, 183
paper (including papermaking), 65–66, 69, 96, 111, 113–14, 117–18, 127, 155, 166
Parthia/Parthians, 25, 30, 45, 55, 58–60, 68, 82–84, 95, 98–99, 103, 154–155, 161, 174, 189
Parthian shot, 13, 60
Pax Romana, 58
Periplus of the Erythraean Sea, 152

Index

Persia/Persian Empire, xiii, 25, 67, 80, 89, 96–97, 100, 142, 166, 192
Persian Gulf, 58, 152
petroglyphs, 186, 190–1
Pharsalia, 62
P'iankov, Igor', 162, 166
Pliny the Elder, 60, 62, 69, 156
podboy (tomb), 78–79
Prophet Muhammed, 193
Protector General of the Western Regions, 47, 86, 100, 117, 155, 175, 182
Ptolemy, Claudius, vi, xi–xiv, 90, 110, 130, 131, 136–39, 141–47, 153–54, 156, 158–59, 161–62, 164–67, 169, 174, 177, 192, 195–96
    accuracy of longitudinal coordinates, 151
    Almagest (Greatest), 139
    Asiatic Geography, 152
    birth of, 138
    Central Asian map of, 170
    coordinate system, 152
    difficulty faced in preparing maps, 142
    error in underestimating Earth's circumference, 144
    Geographia (see *Geographia*)
    Geographike Hyphegesis, 143
    hormeterion, 165
    issue of longitude, 150
    landmark on old Silk Road, 104, 170, 176, 184, 188,
    method of gathering information, 142

Septima Asiae Tabula (Seventh Map of Asia), 144, 171
Stone Tower, 84, 144, 148, 149, 151–52
study of ancient geography and cartography, 170
System of Astronomy, 139

Qilian Mountains, 46, 74
Qin Dynasty, 6, 8, 18
Qin, Emperor, 33

Rabatak Inscription, 86, 90
Rajatarangini, 105–6
Ramayana, 74, 127
Rapin, Claude, 170, 172
Rawlinson, Henry, 110, 131, 167
Records of the Grand Historian. See *Shiji*
Red Sea, 58, 152
Renaissance, 57, 145, 147, 172
Res Gestae, 165
Rhodes, 142, 149–150, 158
Richthofen, Ferdinand von, 4, 46
Ritter, Carl, 170
Rolfe, J. C., 166
Roman Empire, 57, 117, 138, 155
Roman legions, 60, 192
Rome/Roman, xi, 25, 13, 58–62, 66, 87–88, 95, 117, 138–39, 142, 154–55, 165, 186
    Antonine Plague, 68
    demand for exotic goods, 60
    import and export of goods from China, 82
    instability, 68
    maritime trade with India, 82

Index   221

silk garments from China, 62
'Tyrian purple' textiles, 154
Roof of the World, xii, 50, 110,
    162, 168, 196
Roxana, Princess, 97
Roy, P. C., 96
Royal Geographic Society, 108,
    130

Saka, tribes, 11, 74, 77, 79, 80–81,
    91, 96–98, 166
Salomon and Marino, 195
Samarkand, 65, 97, 120, 137, 161,
    174, 182
Sand-Buried Ruins of Khotan, 110
Sanskrit, 34, 92, 103, 105–6
Sarikol, kingdom, 110
Sasanian invaders, 68
Seleucid Empire, 80, 98
Seleucus, General, 98
Seneca (Roman philosopher), 61
Sera metropolis (Chinese capital),
    149, 151, 153, 158, 166–67
Seres (China), vi, 3, 62, 94, 110,
    153–54, 156–58, 164, 166,
    176
sericulture, 3, 62, 65, 112–13
Serindia (book), 123
Serindia (Chinese Turkestan), 94
Shamanism, 13
Shanyu (supreme leader of
    Xiongnu), 13, 15, 18–22,
    24–25, 36, 41, 75, 78, 175
Shentu (ancient India), 27
Shiji, 5, 7–9, 12, 14, 17, 19, 24,
    26, 29, 37, 45, 52, 74, 78, 81,
    83, 96, 98–99, 188–89, 193

silk bales and thread, 3, 18, 62–63,
    58, 117, 171
silk export, from China, 29
silk garments and colouring of, 62,
    154
silk industry, in Khotan, 113
silk, production of, 62–63
Silk Road, xi–xiv, 4, 9, 26, 31,
    46–47, 52, 54, 55, 56–70,
    82, 84, 88, 90, 93–94, 95, 99,
    104, 106, 110, 116, 119–20,
    135–38, 153–55, 164, 167,
    169, 173, 178, 185–86, 188,
    189, 190, 195–96
    Belt and Road Initiative (BRI),
        69
    birth of, 4, 56
    building of new Silk Road, 69
    economic and political control
        of, 88
    First Silk Roads Era, 56, 63,
        67–68, 82, 94, 95, 189
    grapevine import, 26
    human traffic along, 65
    items traded, 63, 65, 120
    itinerary of, 154
    legacy of, 67
    lingua franca of, 99
    map of, 2
    Maritime Silk Road, 69, 153
    middlemen of, xiii, 58, 70, 82,
        84, 93–94, 154, 189
    movement of people along, 68
    as Paper Route, 65
    Ptolemy's landmark on, 104
    refugees, 65, 67
    Second Silk Roads Era, 68

slaves, 51, 63–65, 67
taxes on caravans, 58
Silk Roads: A New History, The, 57
Silk Roads: A New History of the World, The, 69
Silk Road Foundation, xii
Silk Road Project, 136
Silk Road Studies, 106, 135
silkworm, 16, 63, 65, 113
Sima Qian, 3–9, 12–15, 22, 26, 28, 40, 42, 74, 81, 98–99, 189
Sims-Williams, Nicholas, 86, 101, 119
slaves/slavery, 7, 10, 14, 18, 51, 63–65, 67, 112, 126
Sogdians, xiii, 44, 66, 70, 79, 85, 94, 174, 182, 189
   Ancient Letters, 102, 118, 195
   caravan routes, 119
   commerce, history of, 99
   fight against Alexander the Great, 97
   graffiti on rocks in upper Indus Valley, 101
   Islamic conquests of, 120
   language, 96
   merchant families living in India, 102
   military might of, 97
   as principal propagators of Buddhism, 101
   relations with Chinese, 119
   Saka invasion of, 98
   trading networks of, 102
Sogdian traders, 73, 95–102, 119
Sogdian Traders, 96, 98, 102
Solomon, King, 186
Solomon's Throne. *See* Sulaiman-Too
Song Dynasty, 42
Son of Heaven, 5, 14, 16, 29, 33
Soter Megas (Great Saviour), 90
Spice Route, 47, 58–59, 153
Spitamenes, 97–98
Stein, Aurel, 103–131, 135, 142, 152–153, 164–68, 173, 179–180, 182–83, 195
   discoveries of, 112
   entry into Tarim Basin, 116
   expeditions of, 107, 109
   finds from around Khotan, 114
   his dogs: Dash I–VII, 107, 118
   on location of Stone Tower, 131, 164, 168
   Mohand Marg, 106
Stevenson, Edward, 146, 161, 200
Stone Tower, vi, xi–xiv, 9, 55, 84, 102, 110, 130–1, 135–36, 144, 148, 150–160, 162, 164–67, 169–78, 183–85, 188–89, 196, 199–200
   location of, 148, 158
   Location of Ptolemy's Stone Tower, The, xii, 172
   Lithinos Pyrgos, 135
   Maes's caravan from Bactria to, 160
   quest to find, 173
   Turris Lapidea, 135, 171
Strabo (Greek geographer and historian), 62, 74, 81, 139
Sulaiman-Too, 172, 176–77, 184–96

Survey of India, 107, 168
Suspended Crossing (Hanging Pass), 77, 85, 101
Syene, 140–141, 158
Syr Darya (Jaxartes), 24, 184

Taichu (Grand Inception) calendar, 6
Tajikistan, xiii, 24, 136 ,165, 196
Tajikistan and the High Pamirs, 168
Taklamakan Desert, 24–25, 48, 53, 107–9, 116, 175, 183, 196
Takt-e-Suleiman (Throne of Solomon), *See* Sulaiman-Too
Taktu, Vima, 85–86, 90
Talas, Battle of (AD 751), 65
Tang Dynasty, 22, 42, 59, 68, 126–127
Tao Jung (Buddhist nun), 127
Tarim Basin, 45–47, 50, 57, 74, 83–86, 91–92, 94, 108, 113, 116, 120, 124, 130, 167, 169, 174–75, 178–79, 182, 188–89, 196
Tarn, W. W., 152
Tashkent, 170, 175–76, 178, 184
Tashkurgan, 101, 110–11, 167–69, 176–79, 181, 184
Tengiz-bai Pass, 182–83
Terek Pass, 172
Terracotta Army, 34
The Silk Road (journal), xii, 197
The Silk Road: Trade, Travel, War and Faith, 119
Thomas, Huw, 168–69, 183
Thomson, J. Oliver, 144–45, 151, 159, 166–67

Thousand League horses, 35–36
Through Asia, 108
Tianzhu (Northwest India), 67, 91, 102
Tien Shan Mountains, 160, 175
Titianus (Maes). See *Maes*
Tocharian, 74
Tooley, R. V., 137, 144
Transoxiana, 96
Tupikova, Irina, 169
Tyre, 62, 97, 154

UNESCO (World Heritage List), 122, 136, 190
Uzbekistan, xiii, 24, 136, 170

Vaissière, Étienne de La, 96, 98–102, 119, 189
von Reden, Sitta, 195
Voyage of Maes Titianos, The, 155

Wakhan Corridor, 110, 162, 168, 174, 180
Waley, Arthur, 35, 64, 128
Walker, Annabel, 129
Wang, Yuanlu, 122, 125–26, 130
warhorses, 36, 41–42
War of the Heavenly Horses (104 BC), 37–41, 190
Watson, Burton, 7–9, 18
Wen Di, Emperor, 17, 35
Western Regions (of China), 9–10, 20, 27–28, 38, 42, 46–48, 52, 63–64, 84–85, 99–100, 106, 112, 117, 120, 155, 175, 184
Whitfield, Susan, 68, 129, 197
Wilcken, Ulrich, 97

Woolley, Leonard, 106
Wu Di, Emperor, 6, 18, 26–27, 37–41, 58, 76, 99
   attacks against northern barbarians, 35
   campaigns against Xiongnu, 18–20, 35–36, 41
   dispatching Zhang Qian to journey West, 22
   expansionist policy based on Zhang Qian's reports, 30
   fascination with heavenly horses and immortality, 32, 37
   first caravans, 45–55
   heqin strategy, 19
   love for foreign items and curios, 55
   as Martial Emperor, 35
   pact with Yuezhi against Xiongnu, 20
   rebuilding of his cavalry, 41
   visit of Wusun ambassadors, 30
   War of the Heavenly Horses (104 BC), 37–41
Wusun, tribe, 17, 28–30, 33, 42, 78–79, 175

Xiyuji (Records of the Western Regions), 111
Xiling Shi (semi-mythical Empress), 3
Xin Dynasty, 9
Xinjiang, 10, 106, 108, 110, 136
Xiongnu Empire, 6, 8, 10–20, 22, 24–29, 33, 35, 39, 41, 46, 63, 74–76, 78–79, 85, 95, 119, 175, 190
   defeat of, 36
   pact of brotherhood, 16
   struggle with Han Dynasty, 19–20
   Wu's dealings with, 18–19, 35–36, 41
Xuanzang, 48, 91–92, 110–12, 125, 165

yabghus, 83–84, 88, 169, 181
Yarkand, 47, 167
Yu-ch'eng, city of, 37–38, 40
Yuezhi, nation/tribe, 15, 20–26, 28, 169, 181
   agricultural settlements, 74
   of Bactria, 90
   defeat by Xiongnu, 75–76
   exodus into Central Asia, 79
   Greater Yuezhi, 76–77
   Han's 'hand of friendship', 25
   Lesser Yuezhi, 76
   map of migration path, 72
   migration of, 73–81
   as pastoral nomads, 74
   split of, 83
   Yuezhi-Kushan, 82, 83, 84, 88, 90–91, 96
Yule, Henry, 49, 131, 152, 161, 164, 168, 170, 199

Zadneprovskij, Y. A., 78, 187, 190, 192
Zerafshan River, 96, 137
Zerafshan Valley, 79

Zhang Qian, xiii, 21–32, 41, 44, 46, 58, 65, 76, 79, 81, 96, 99, 186, 188
  account in *Shiji*, 81
  appointment as
    Colonel of the Guard, 28
    general of palace attendants, 29
    Grand Messenger, 30
    subordinate commander, 28
  assistance from king of Ferghana, 24
  captivity of, 24
  death of, 30
  defeat in engagement with Xiongnu, 28
  delivering Emperor Wu's message to Yuezhi, 24–25
  engagement with Wusun and Xiongnu, 28
  expedition reports, 30
  introduction of grapes into China, 65
  journey West, 21–31
  map of journey to Central Asia, 23

Zoroaster, teachings of, 96, 188

Zoroastrianism, 67, 79, 89